Flowers
Colo ring
Book

Take your time to enjoy meditational, stress relieving coloring.

Express the moments in your own vision or take inspiration and practice coloring your skills

BP Coloring Books

Color Test Area

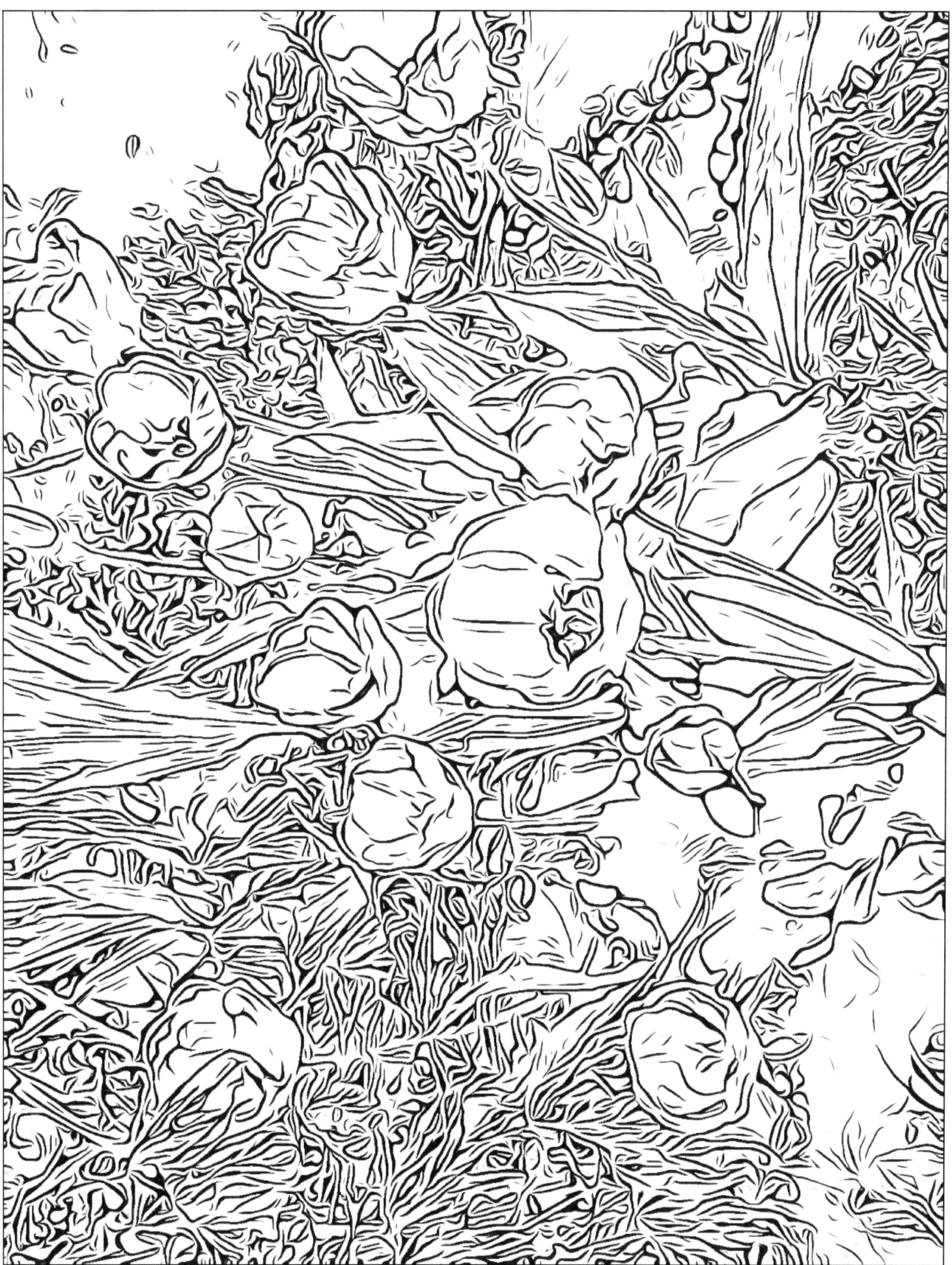

Color Test Area

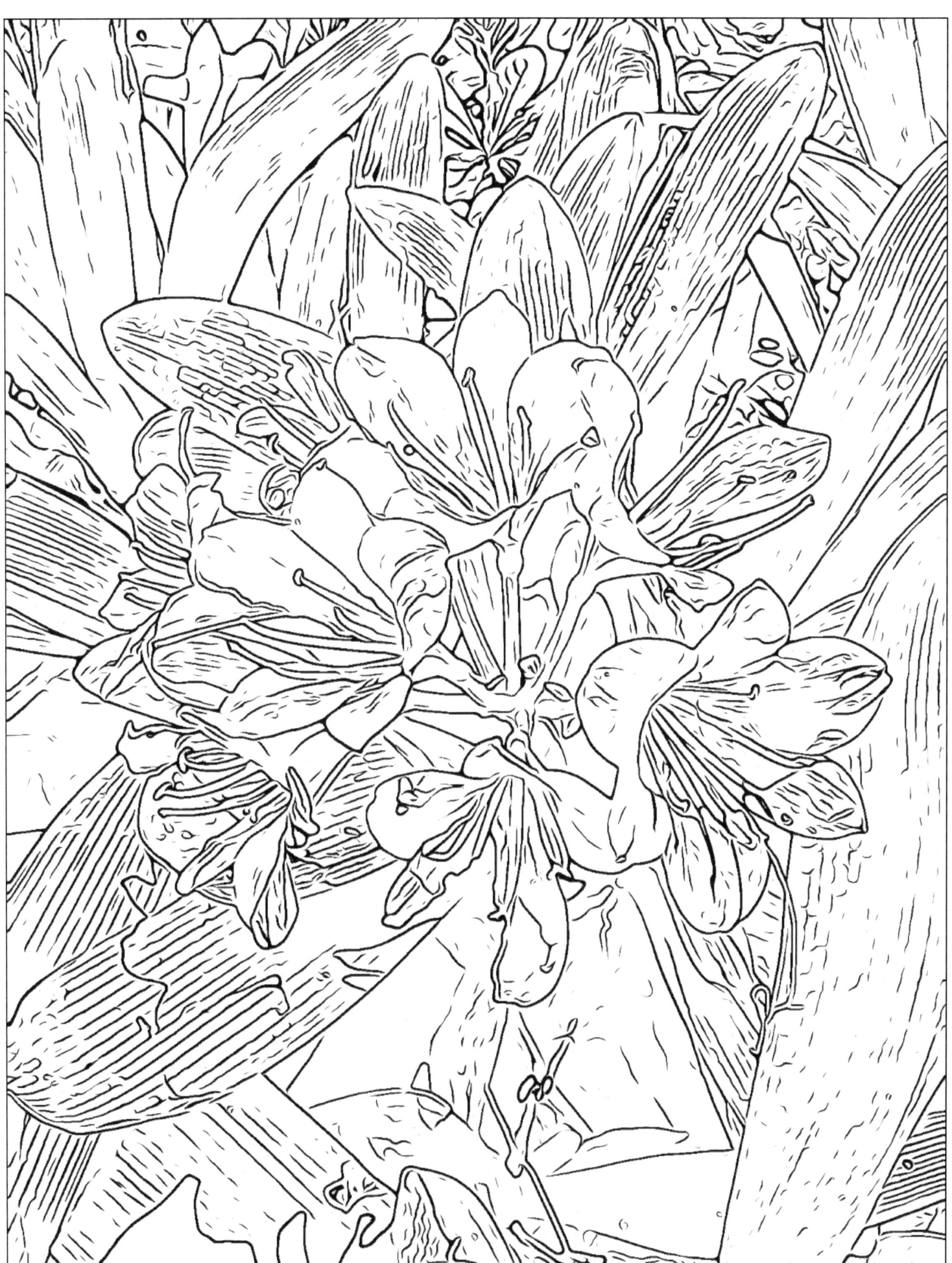

Color Test Area

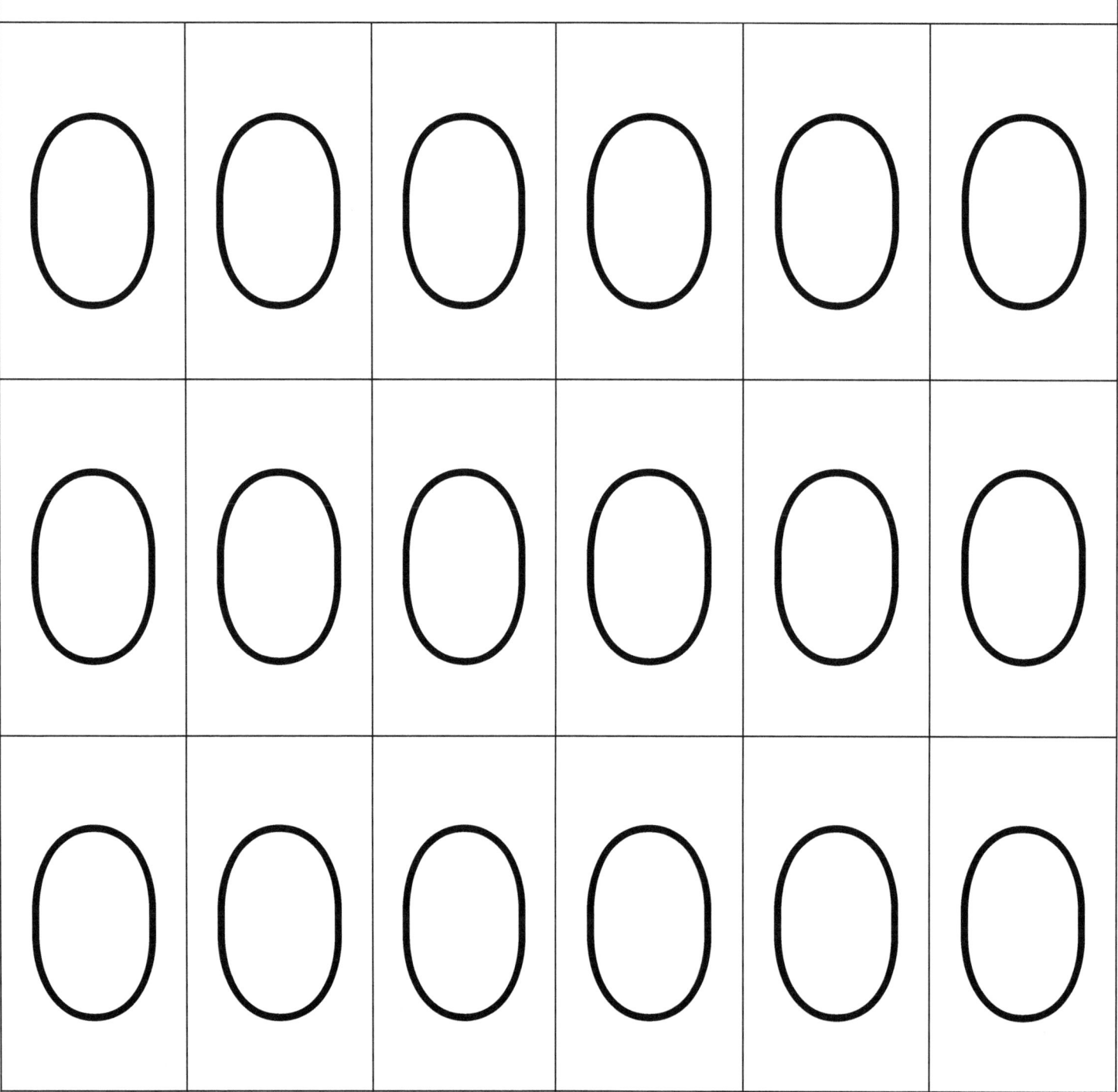

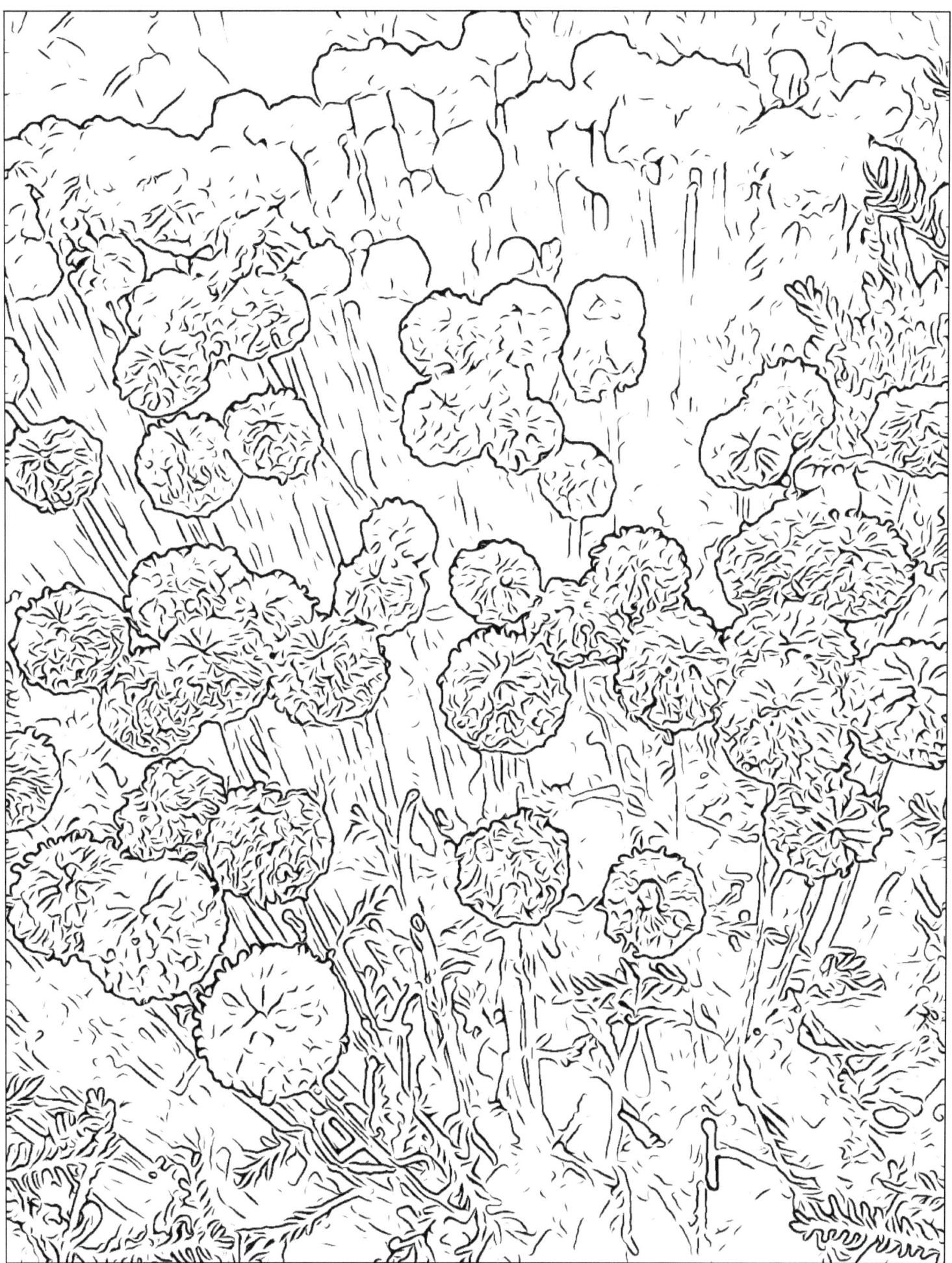

Color Test Area

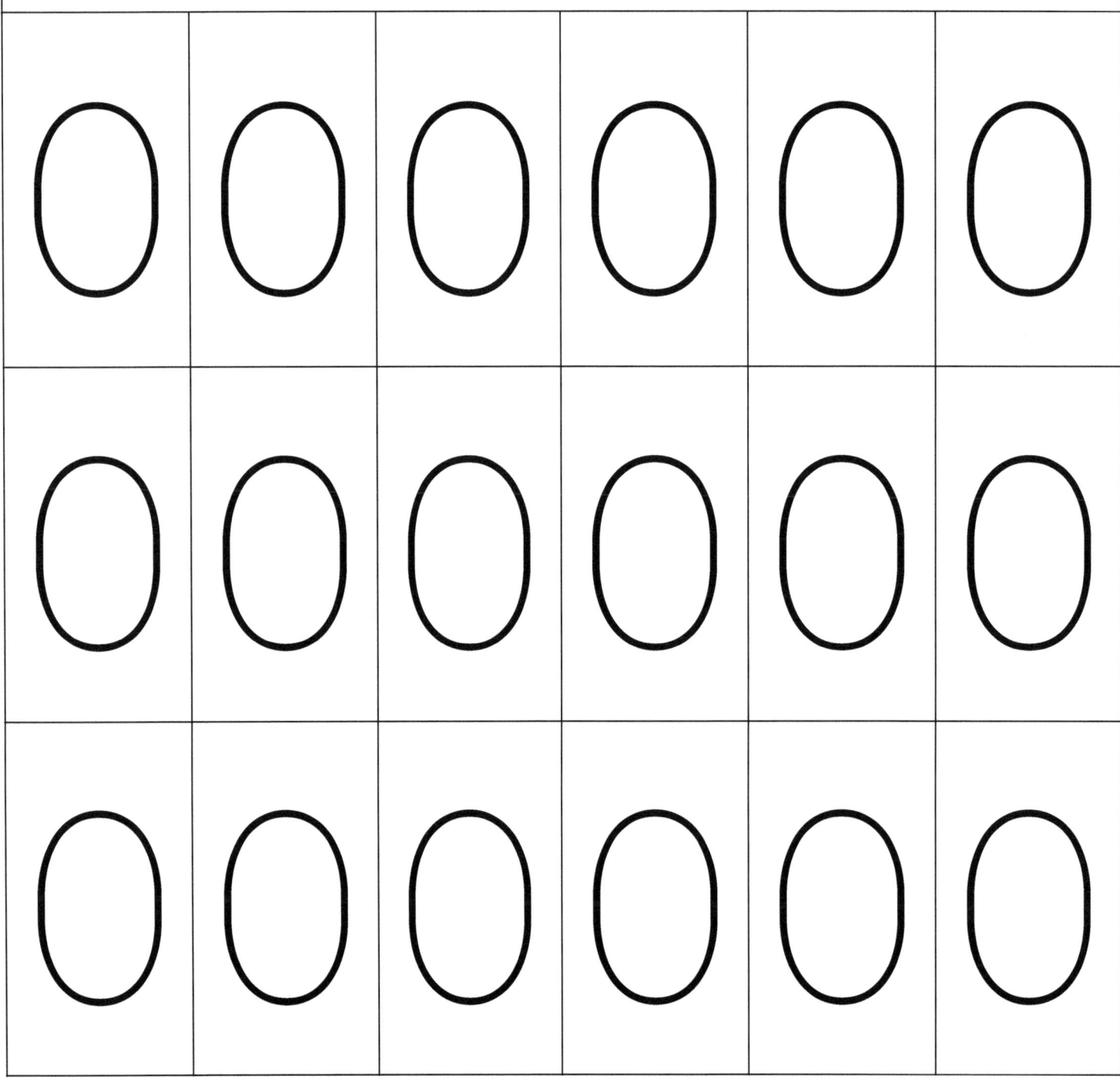

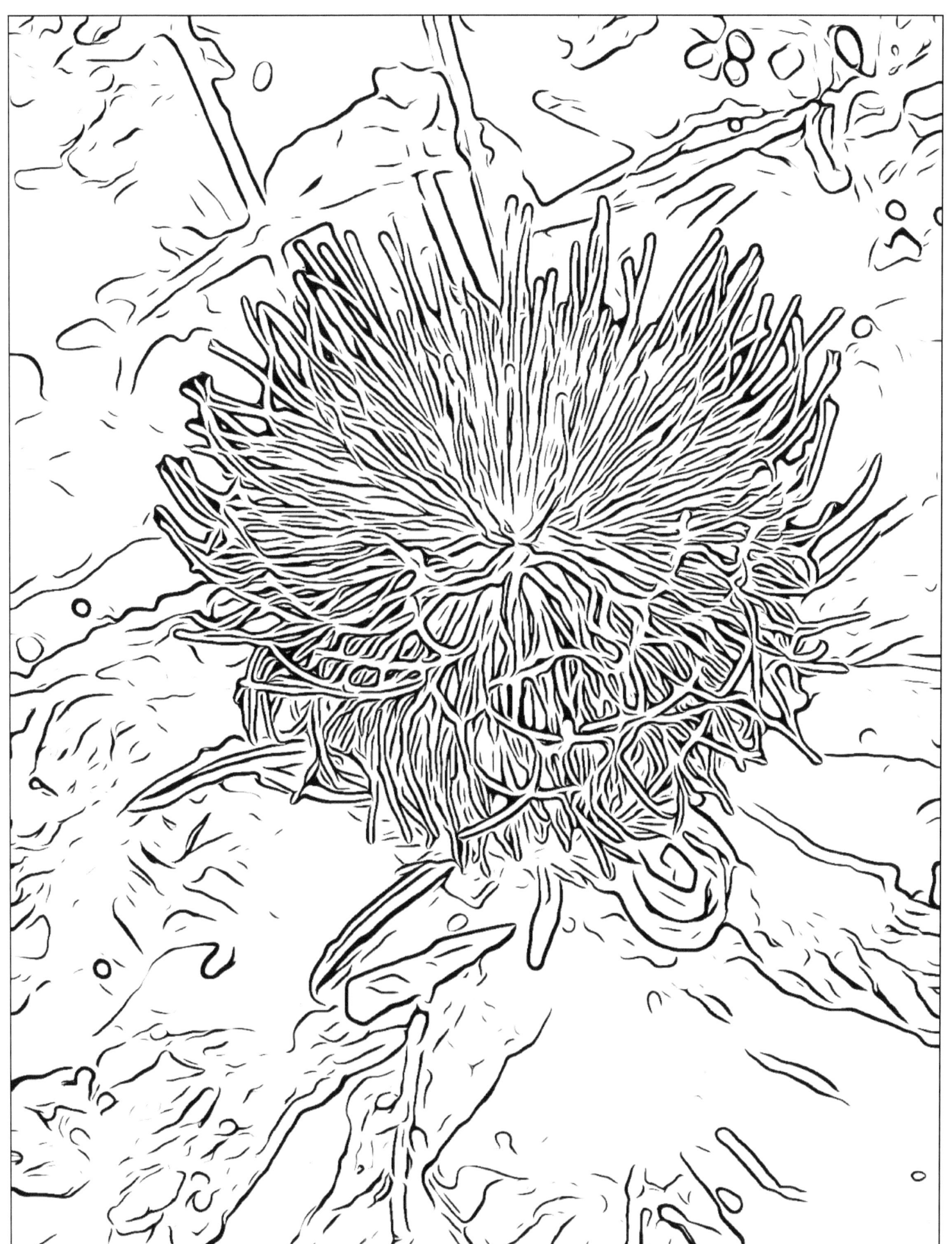

Color Test Area

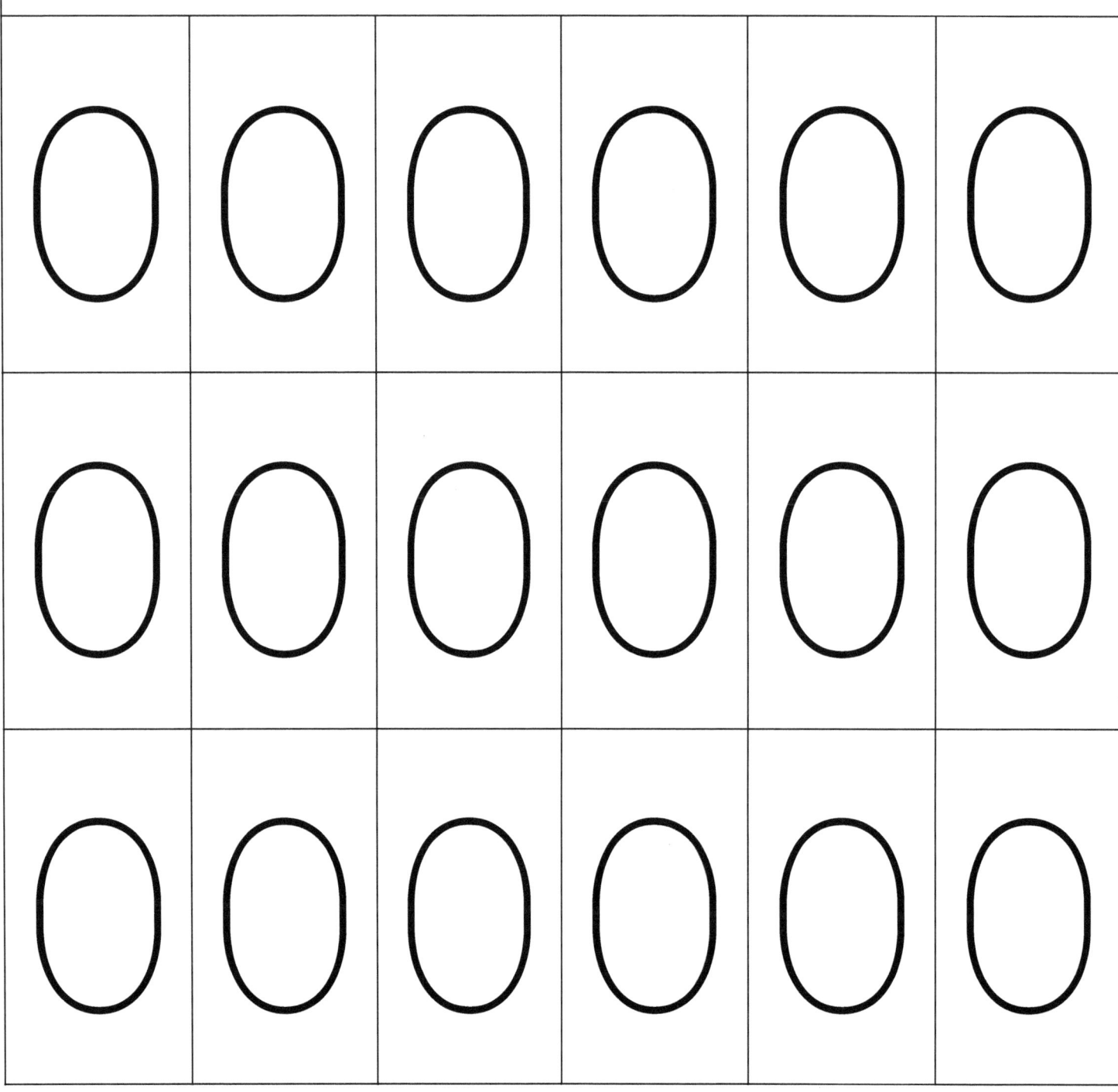

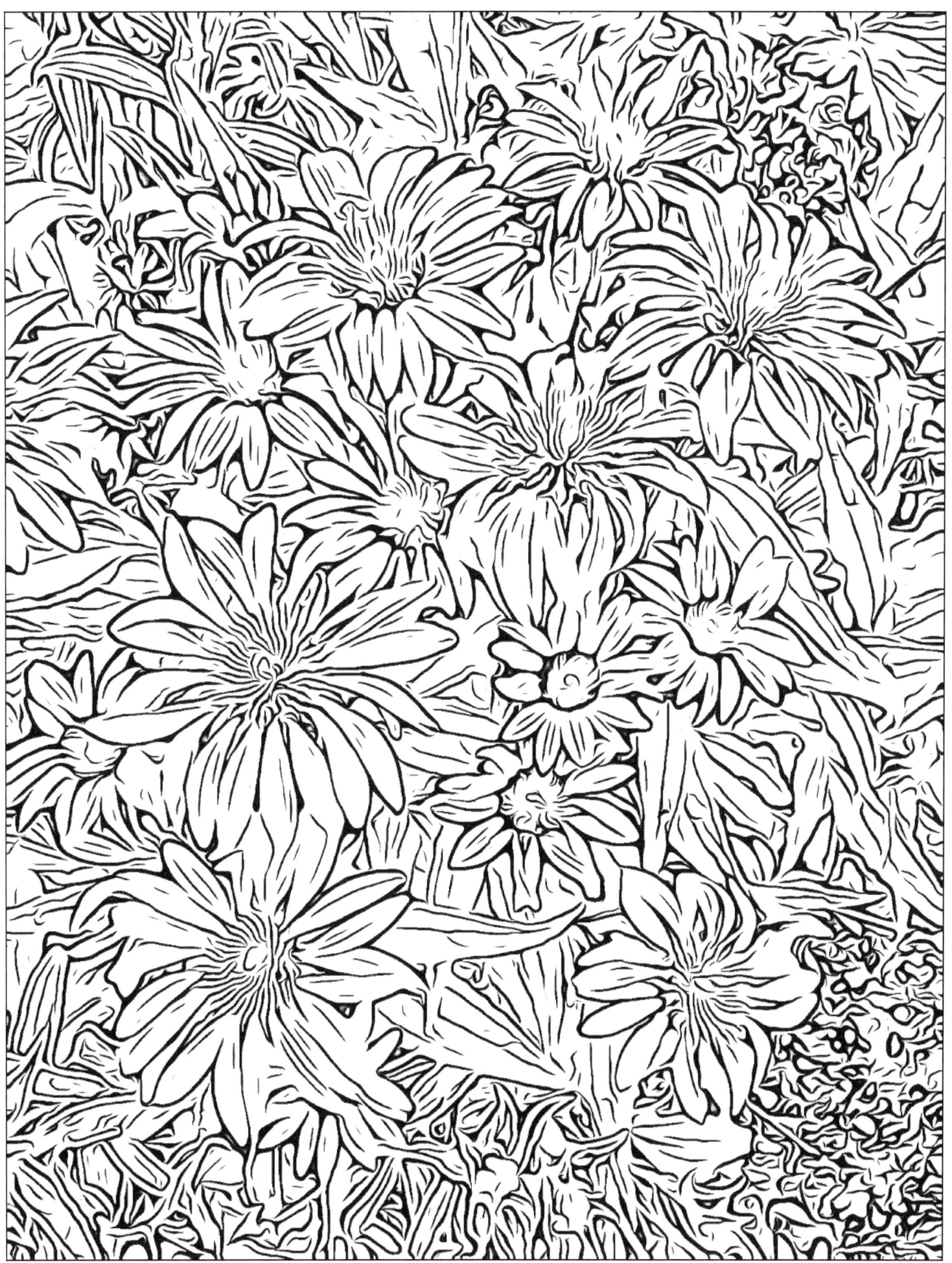

Color Test Area

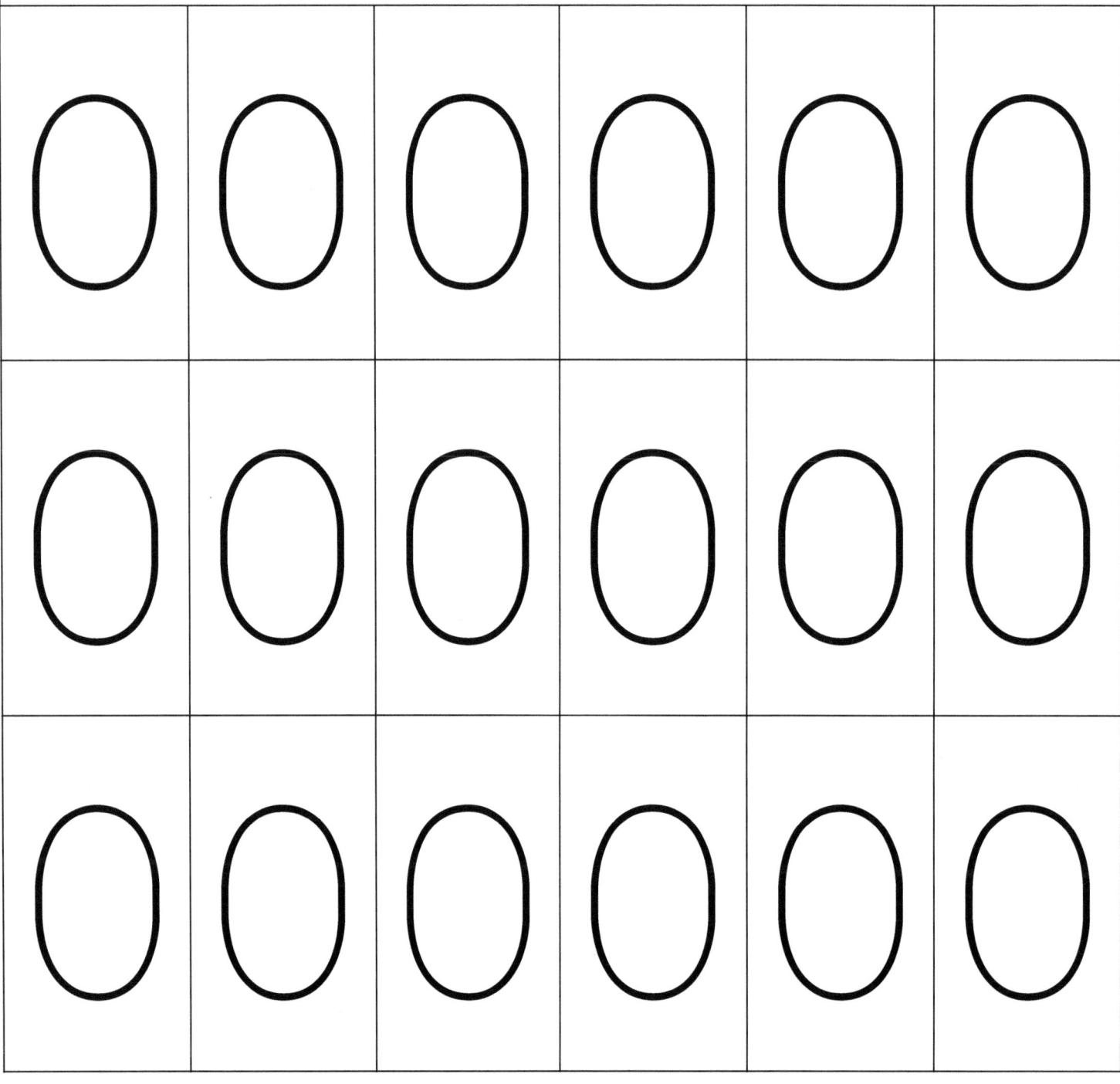

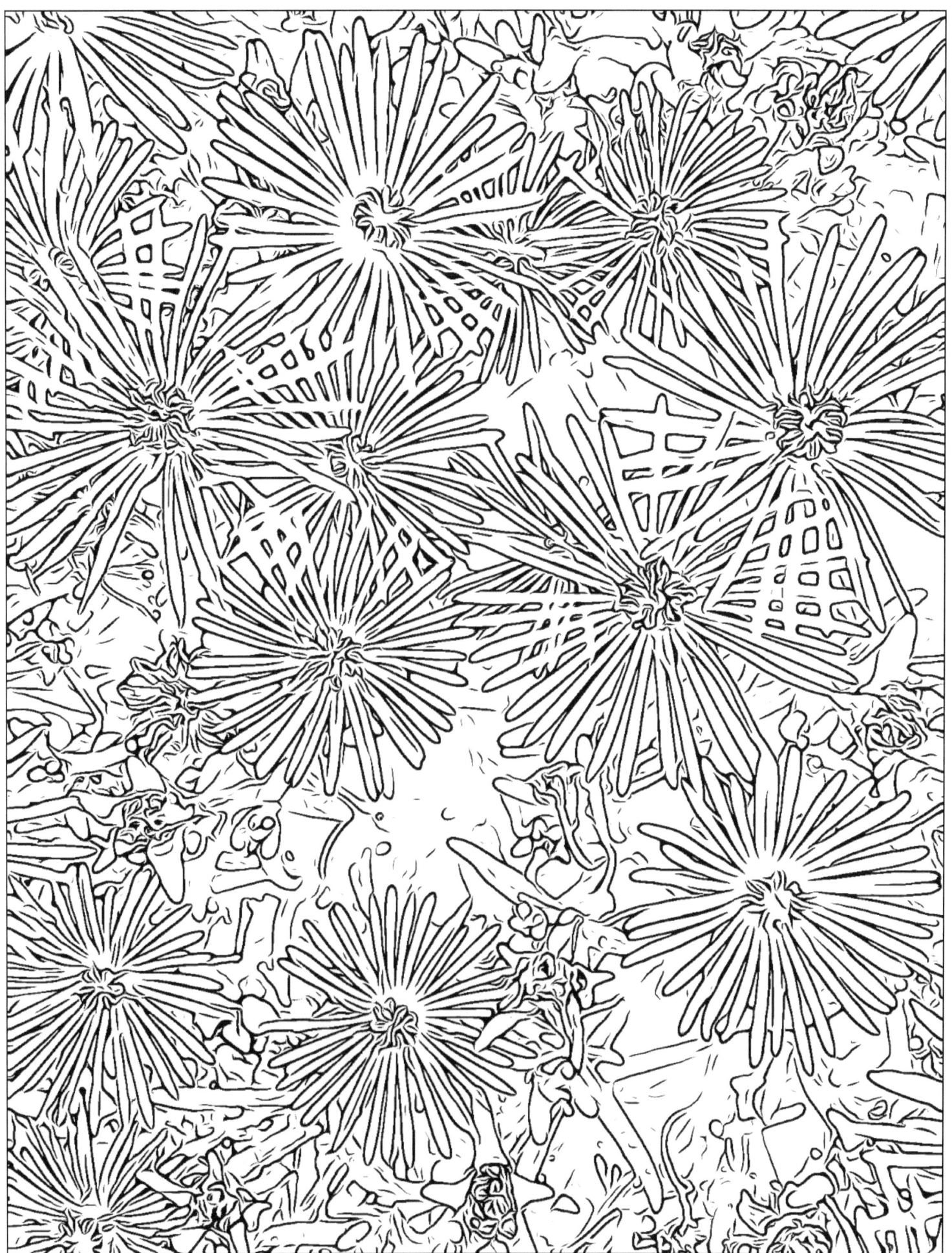

Color Test Area

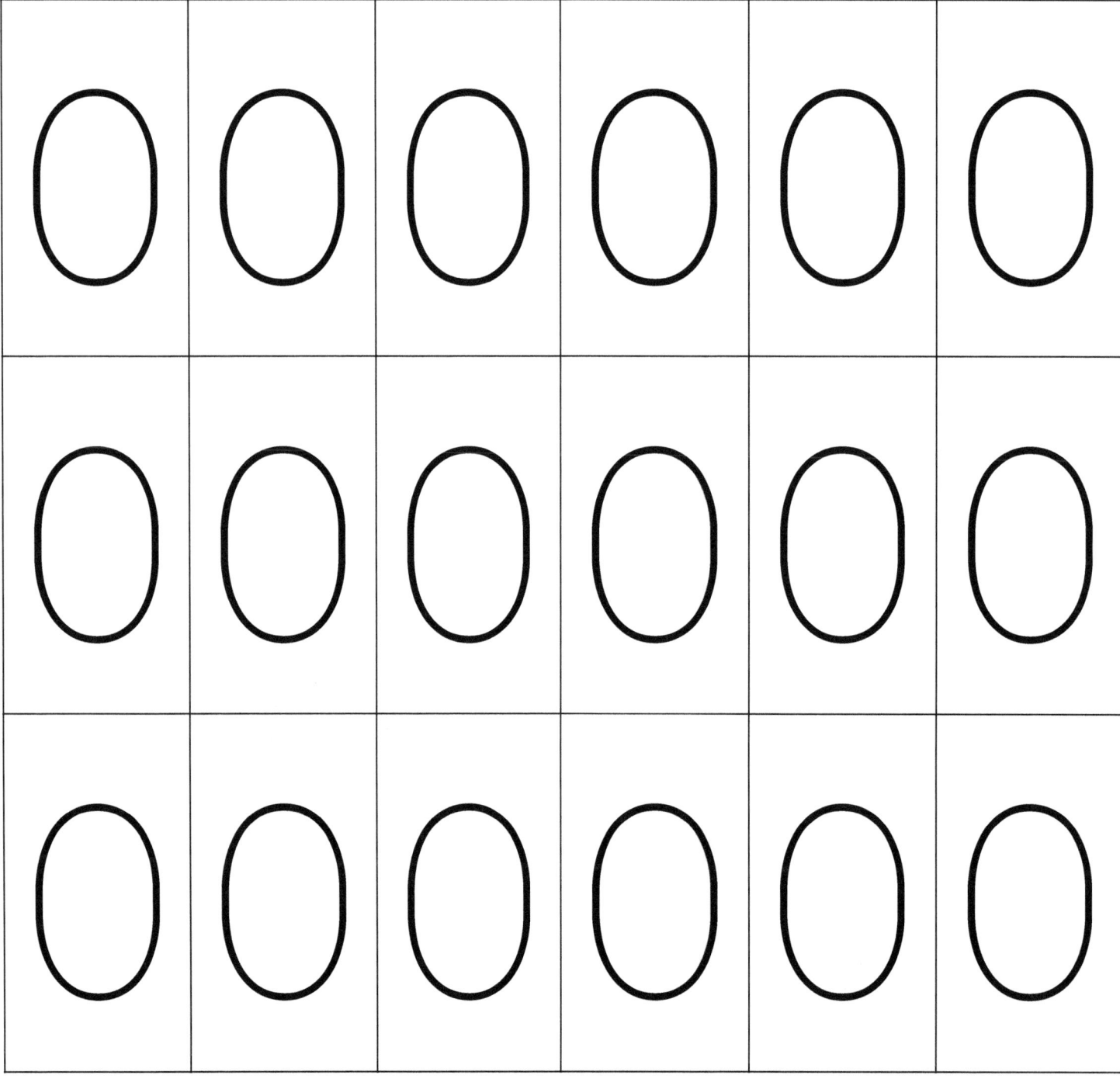

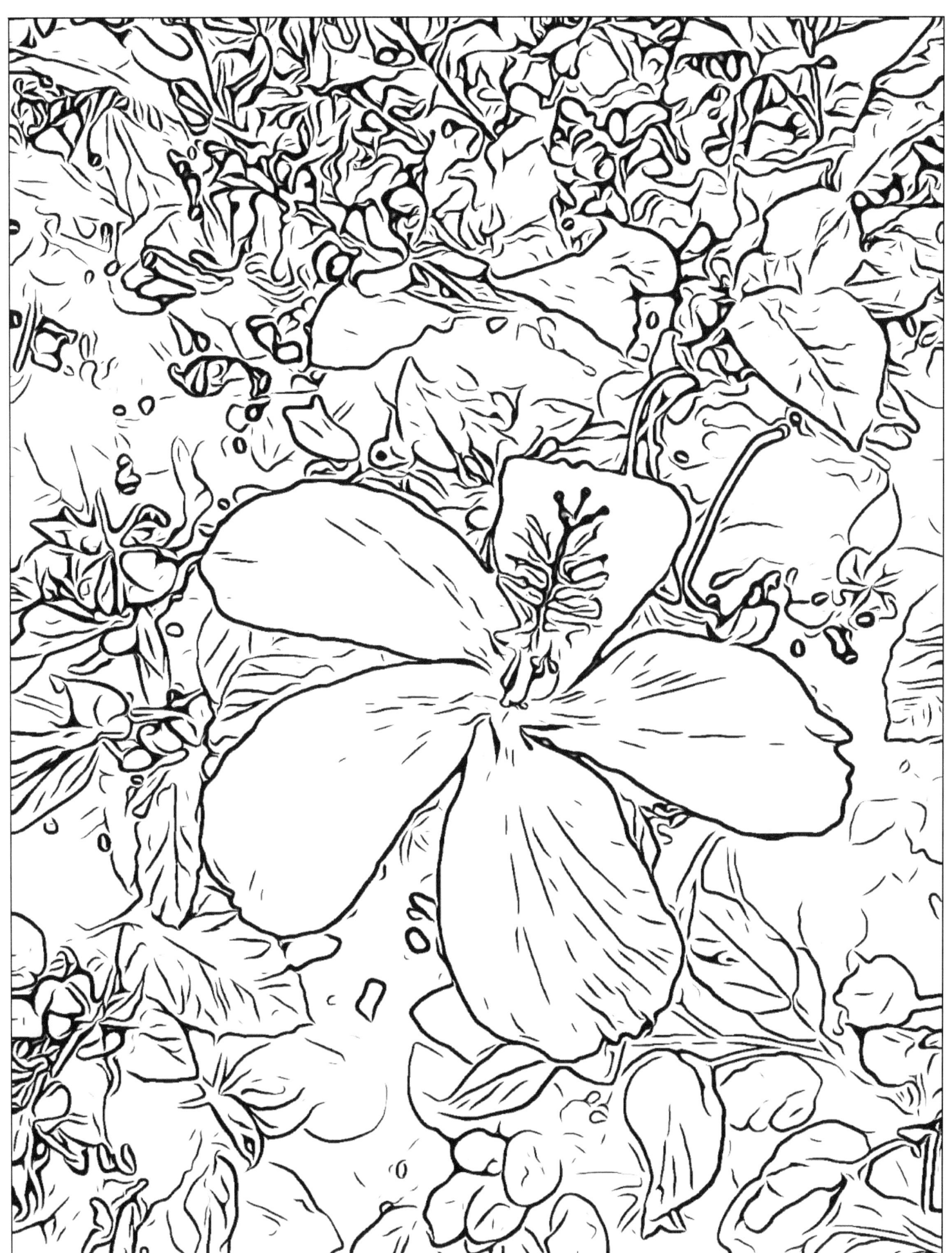

Color Test Area

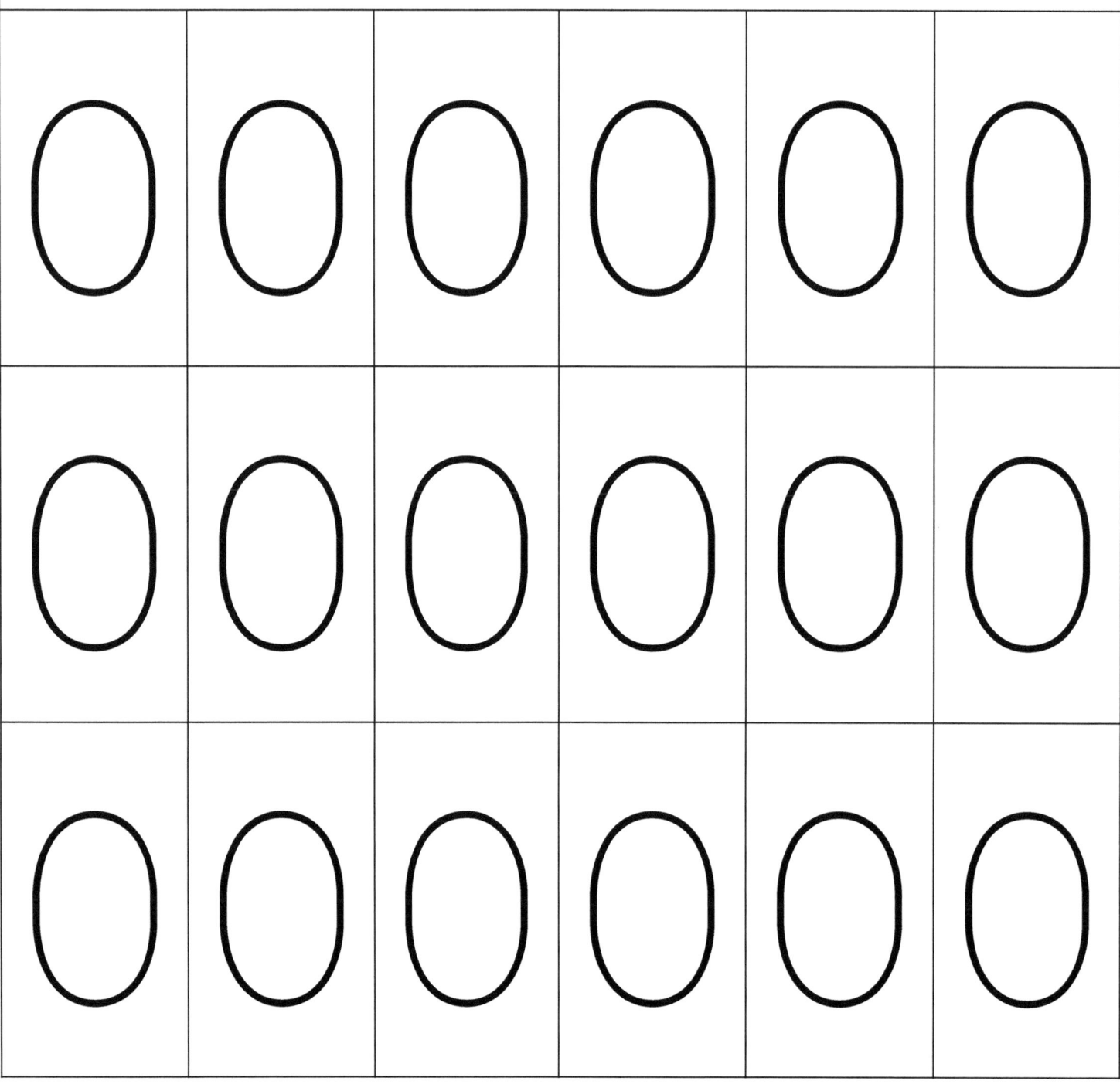

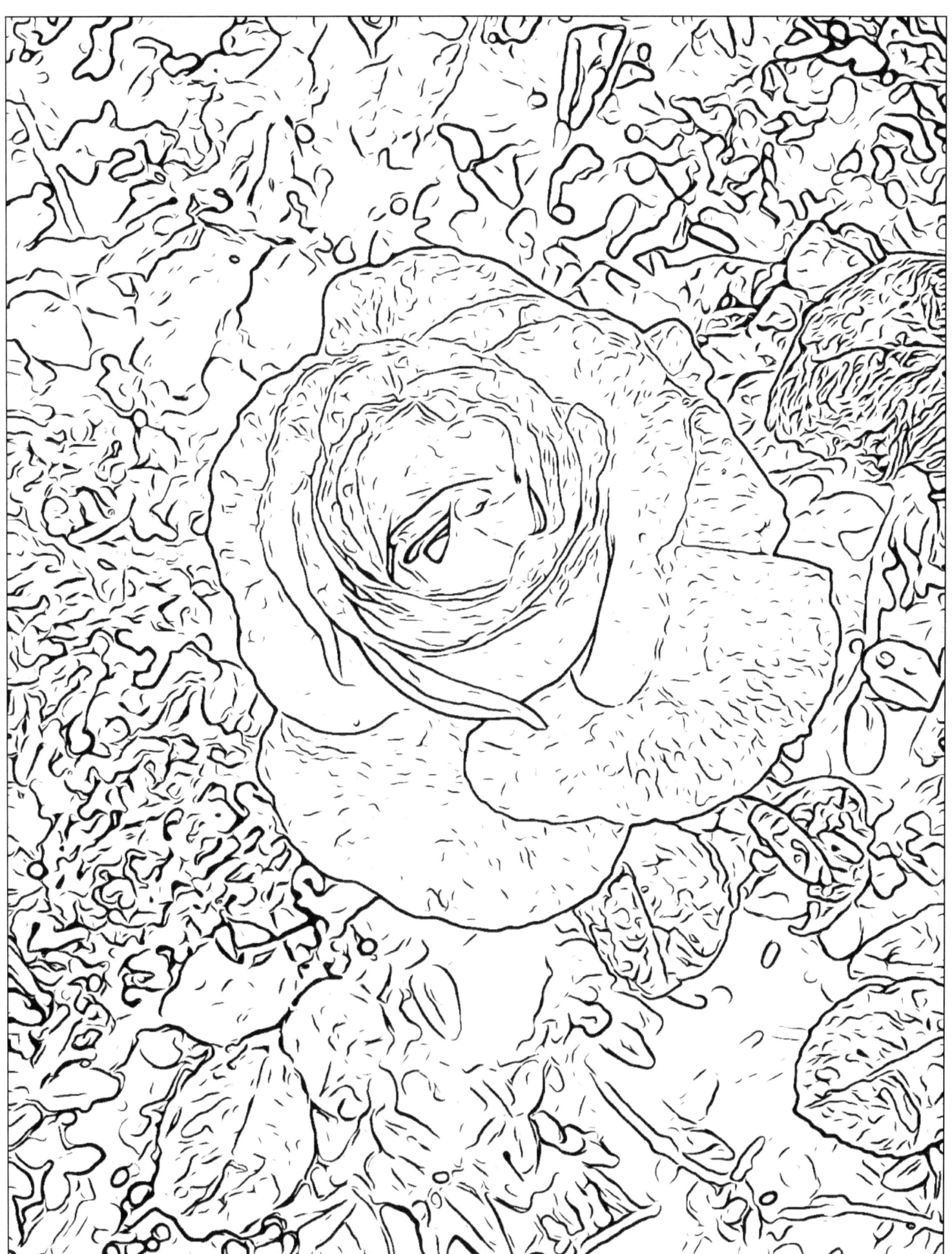

Color Test Area

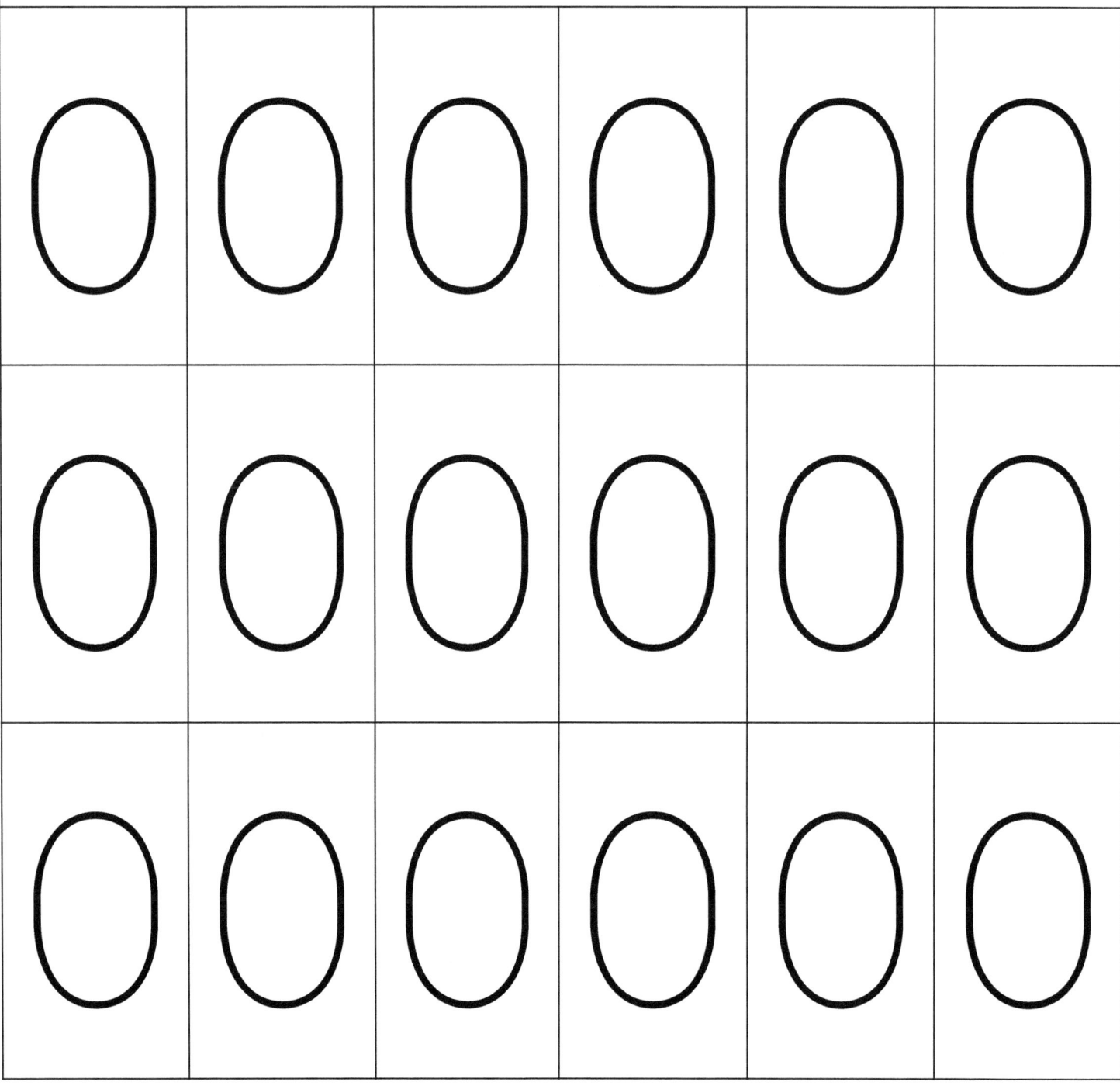

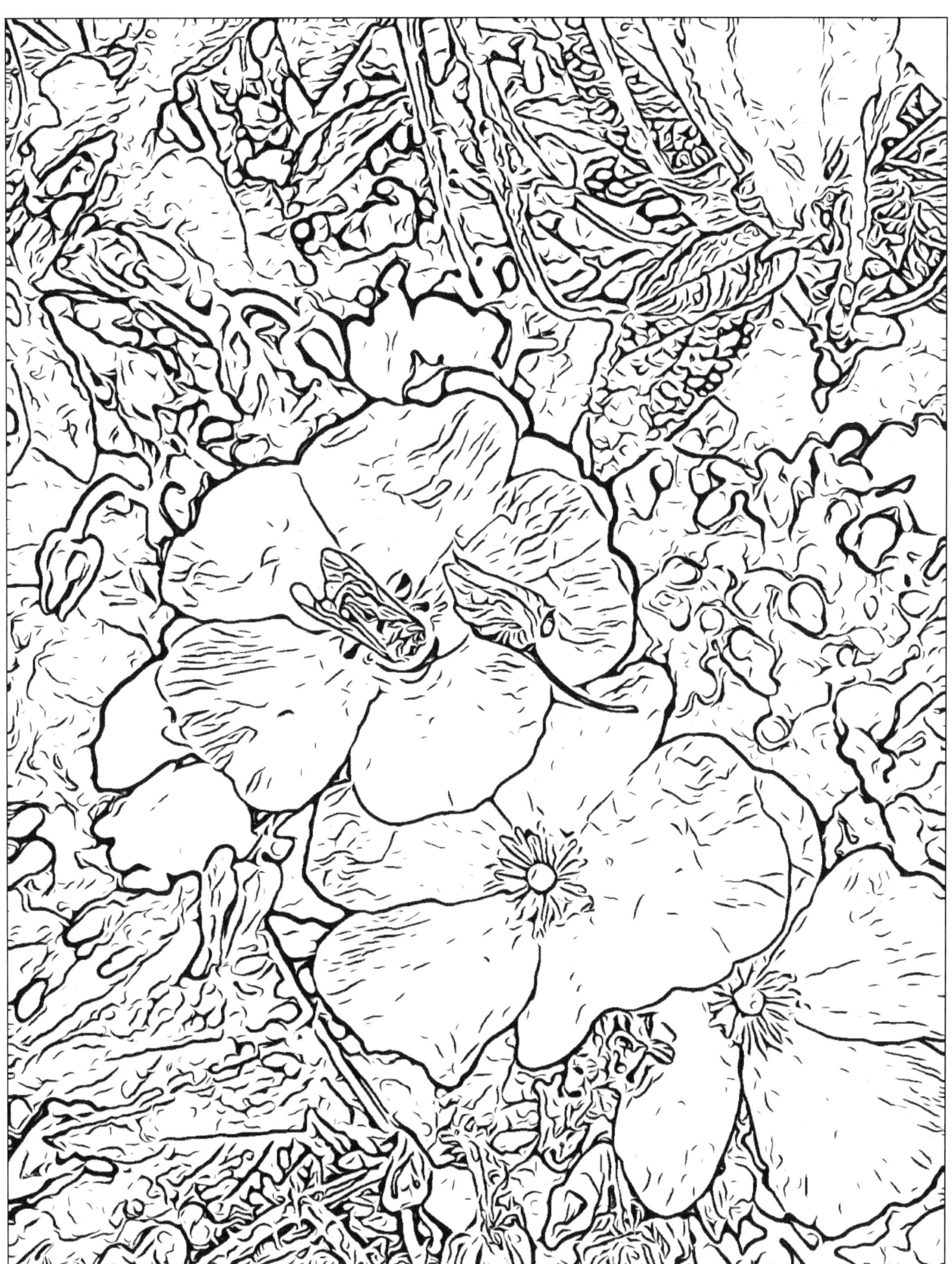

Color Test Area

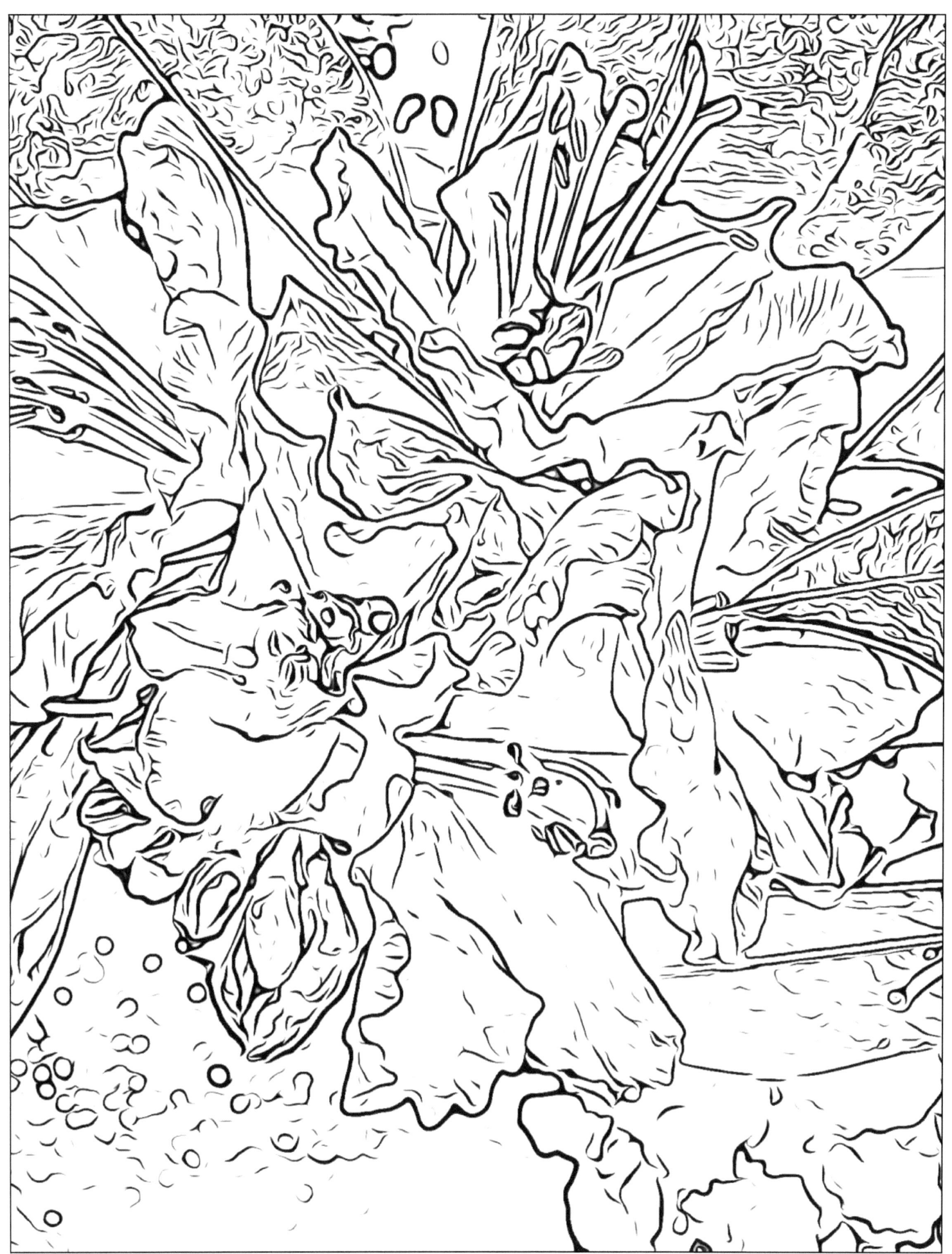

Color Test Area

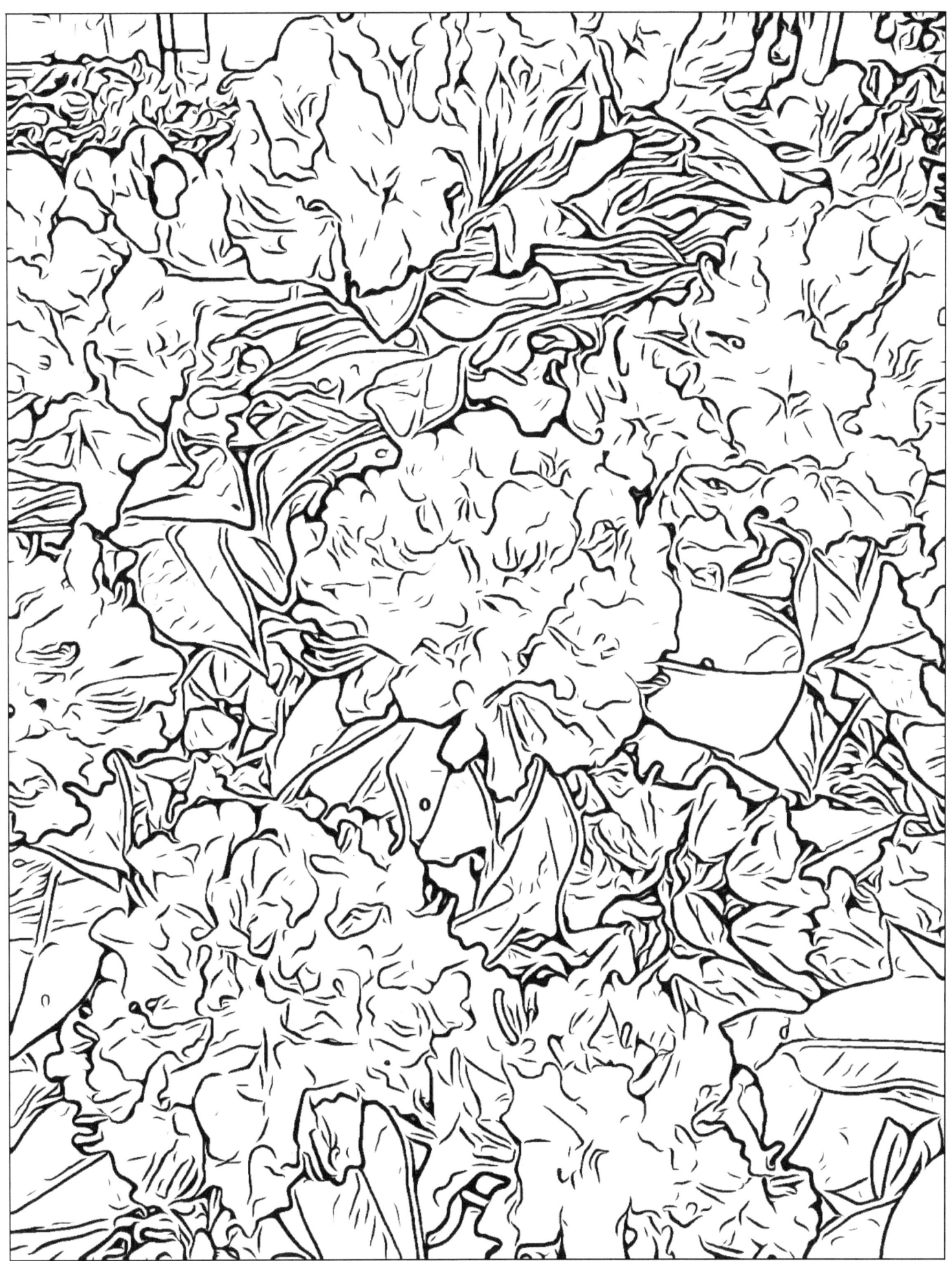

Color Test Area

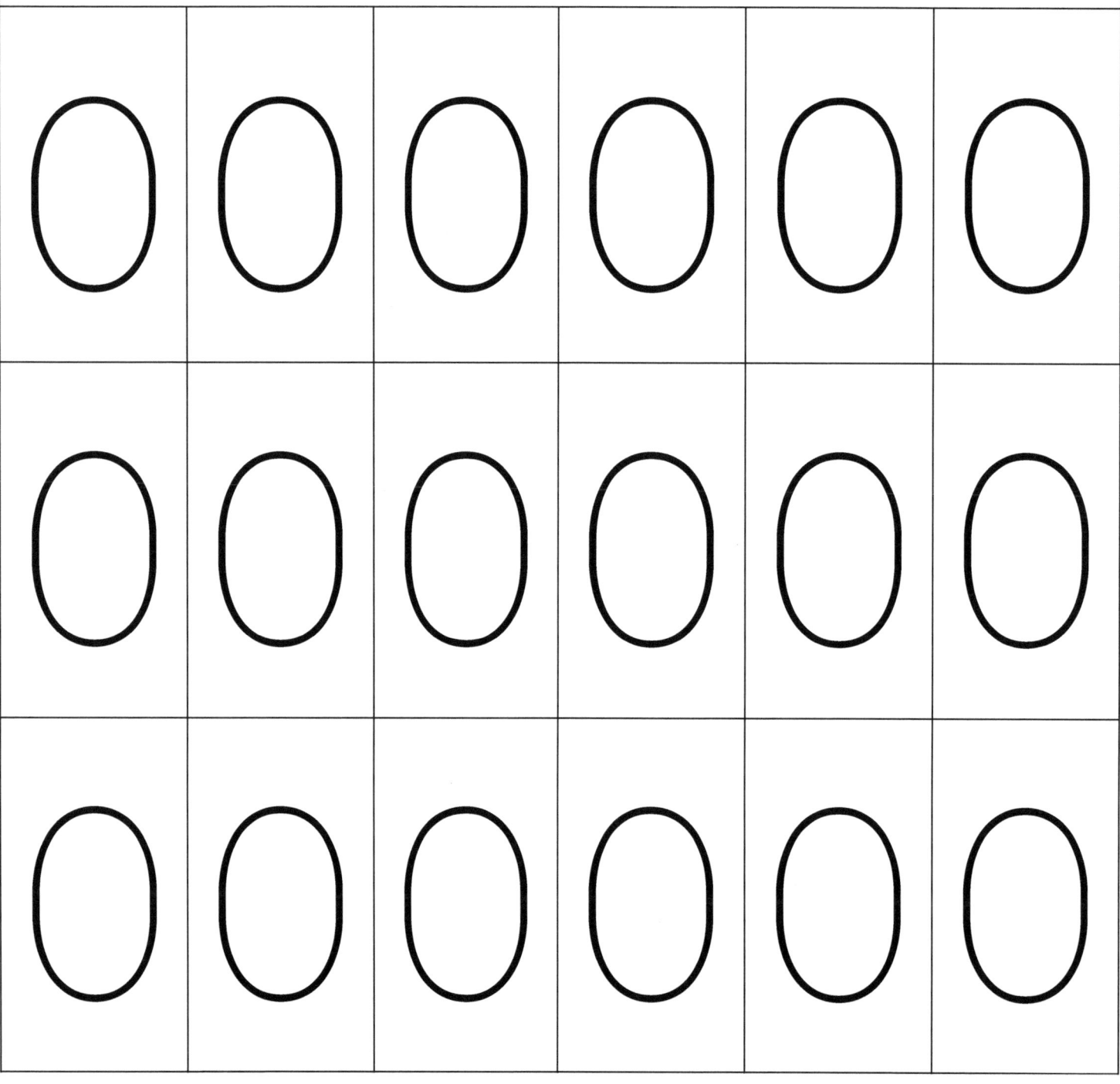

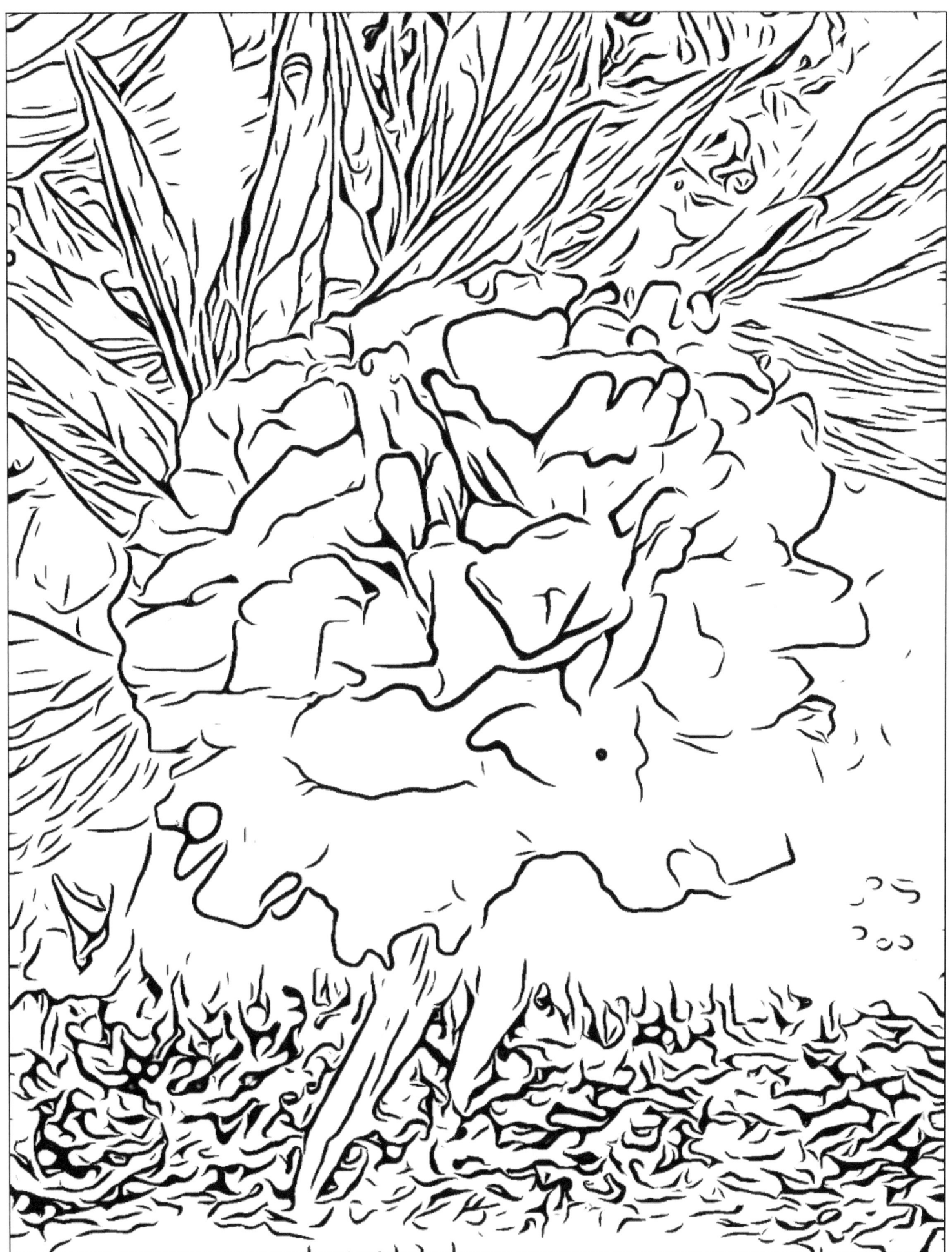

Color Test Area

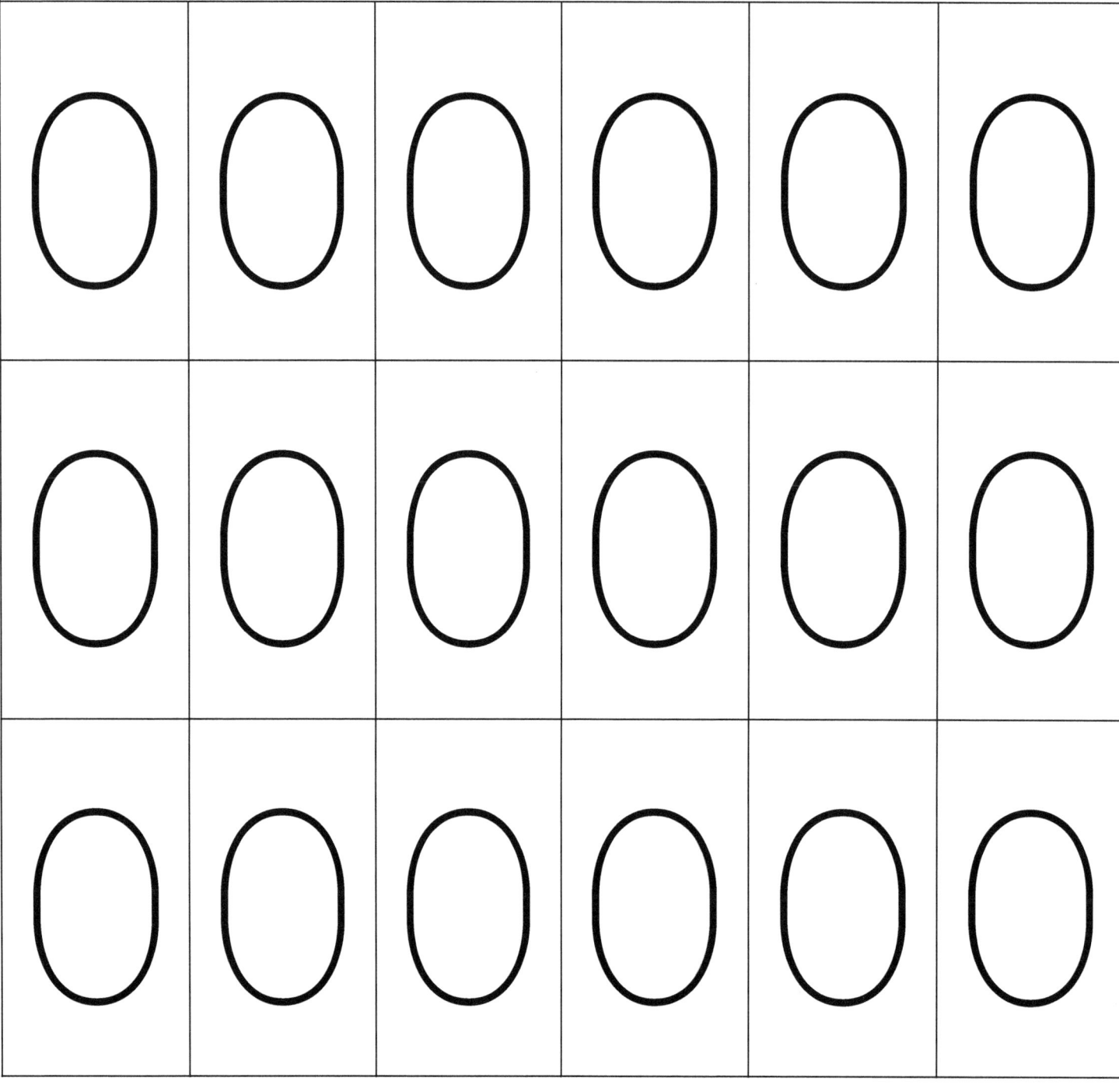

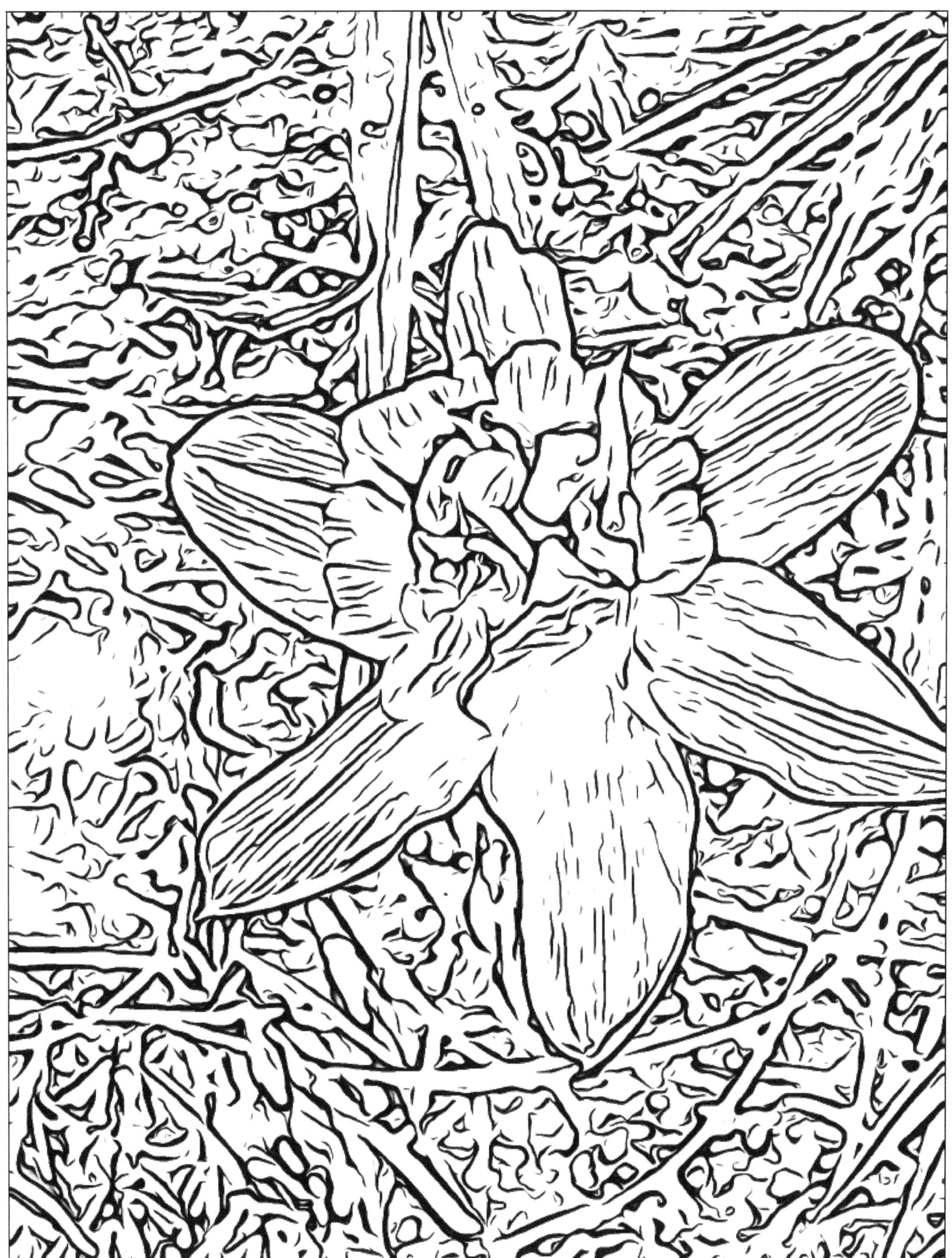

Color Test Area

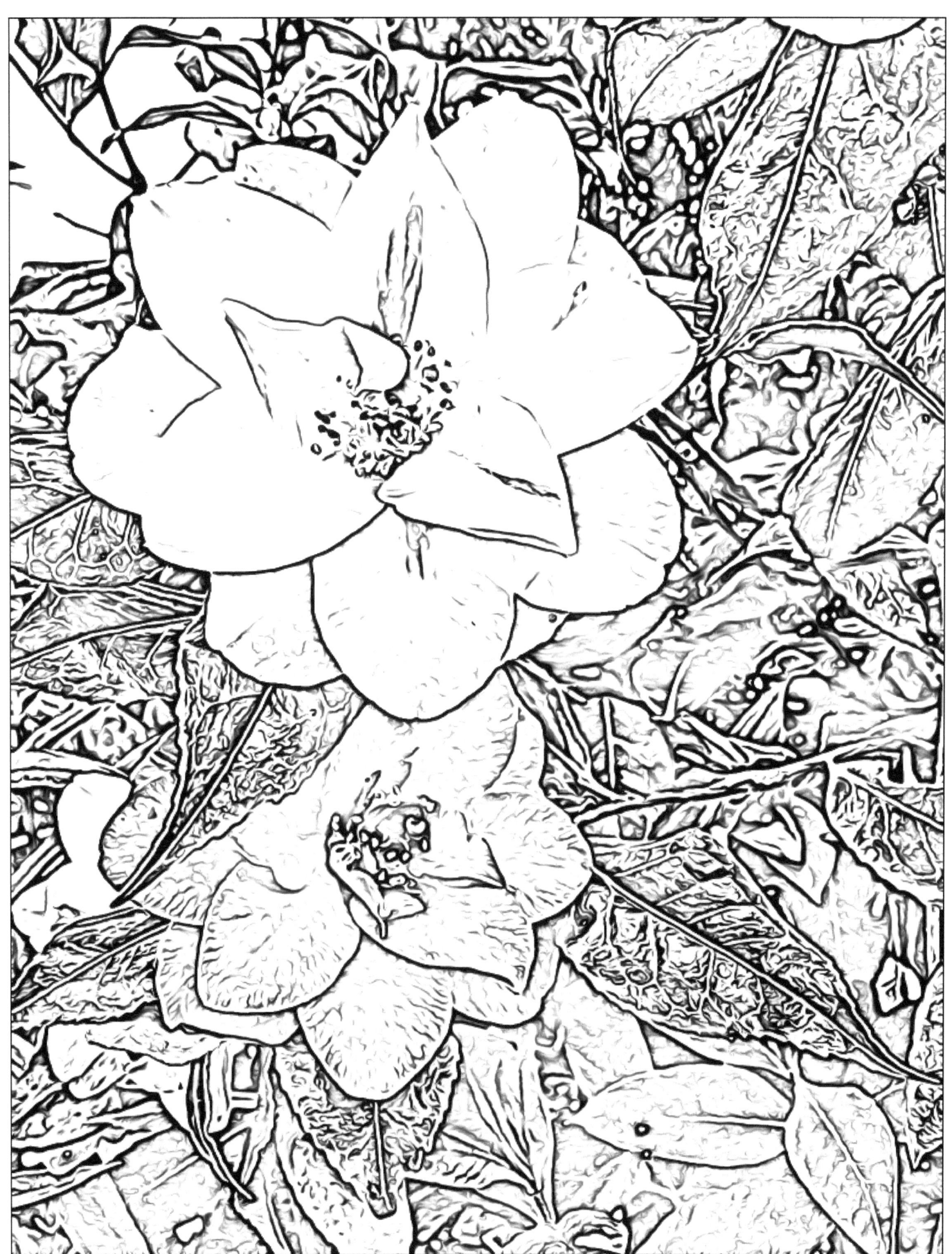

Color Test Area

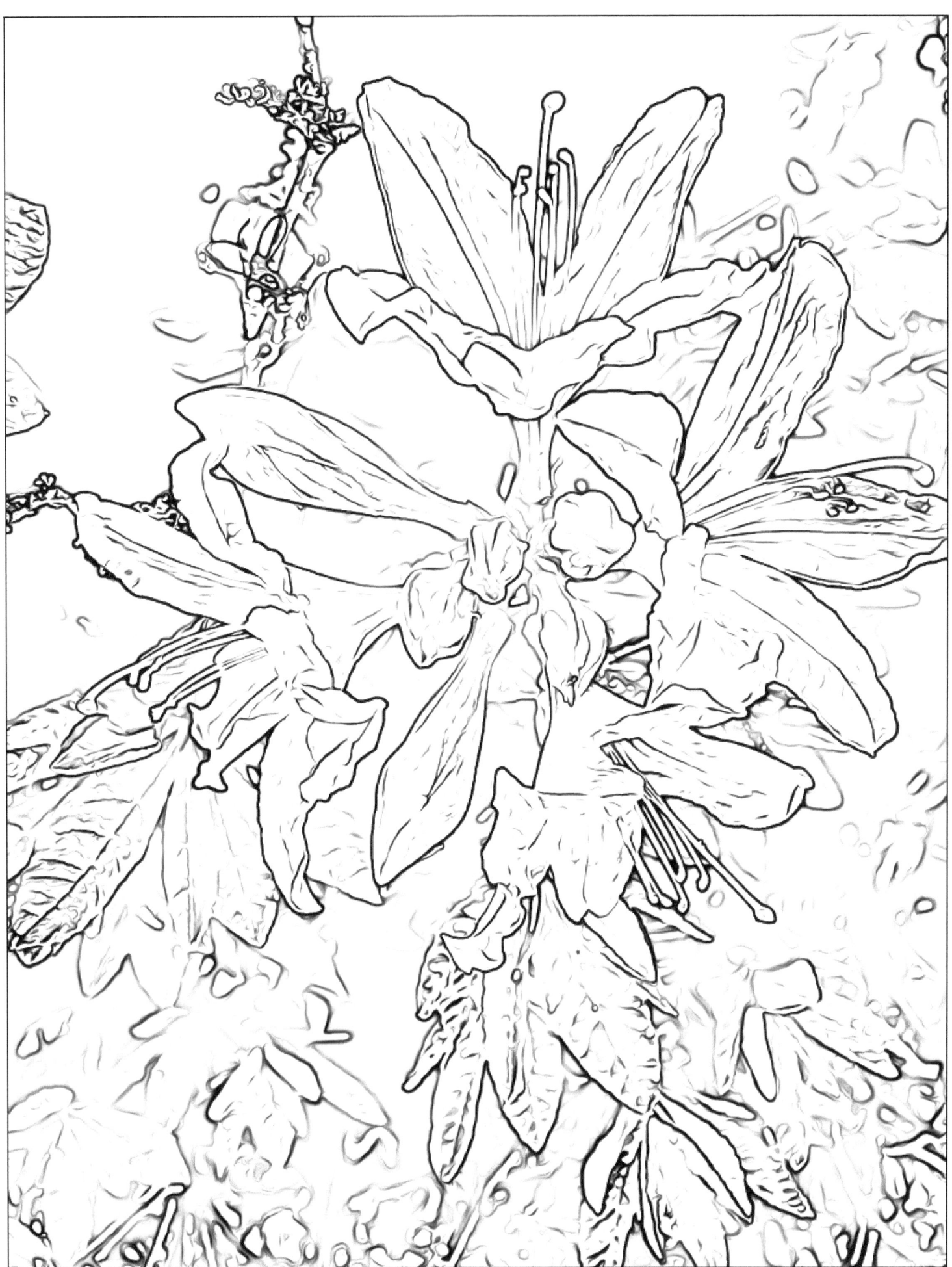

Color Test Area

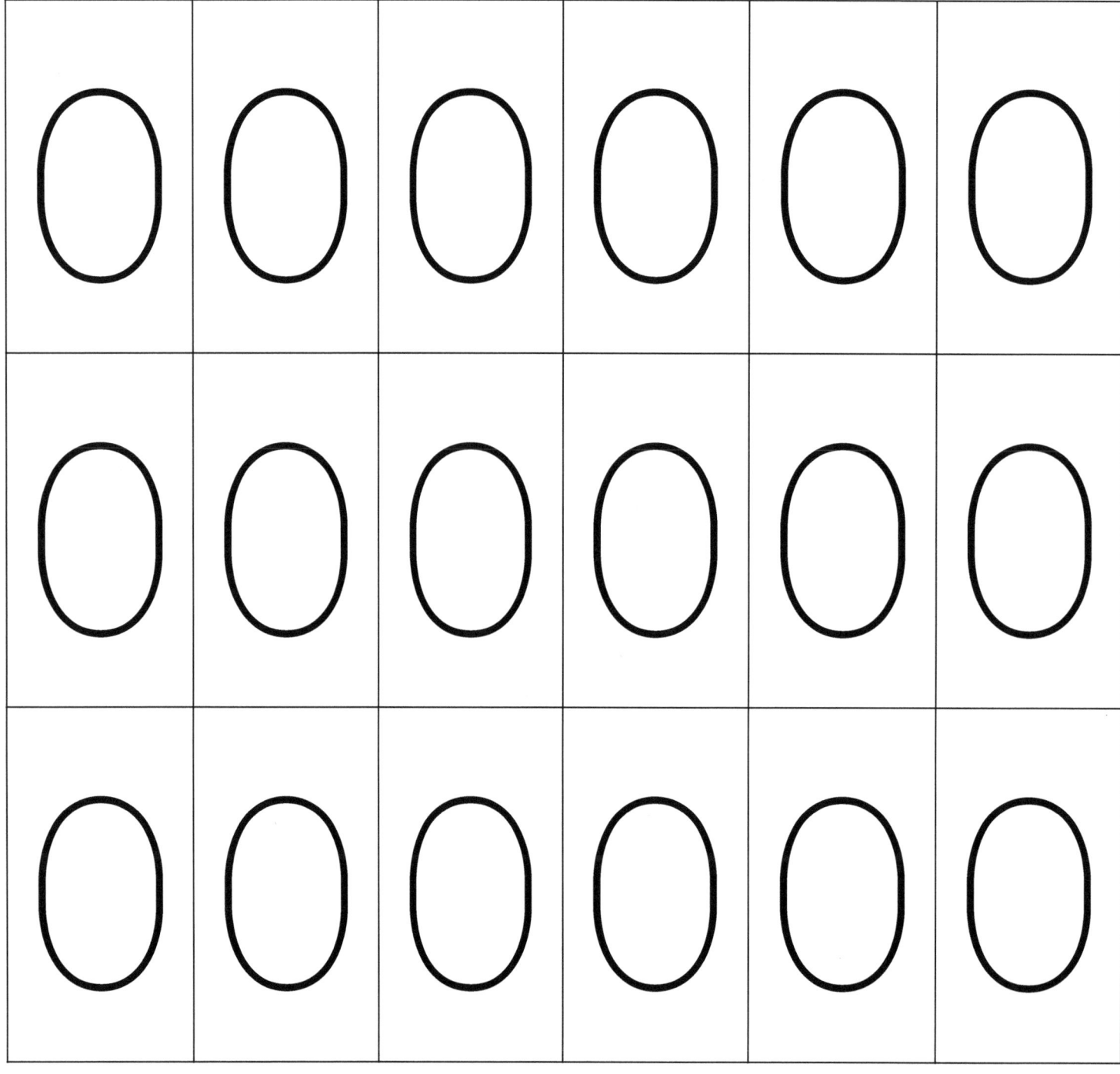

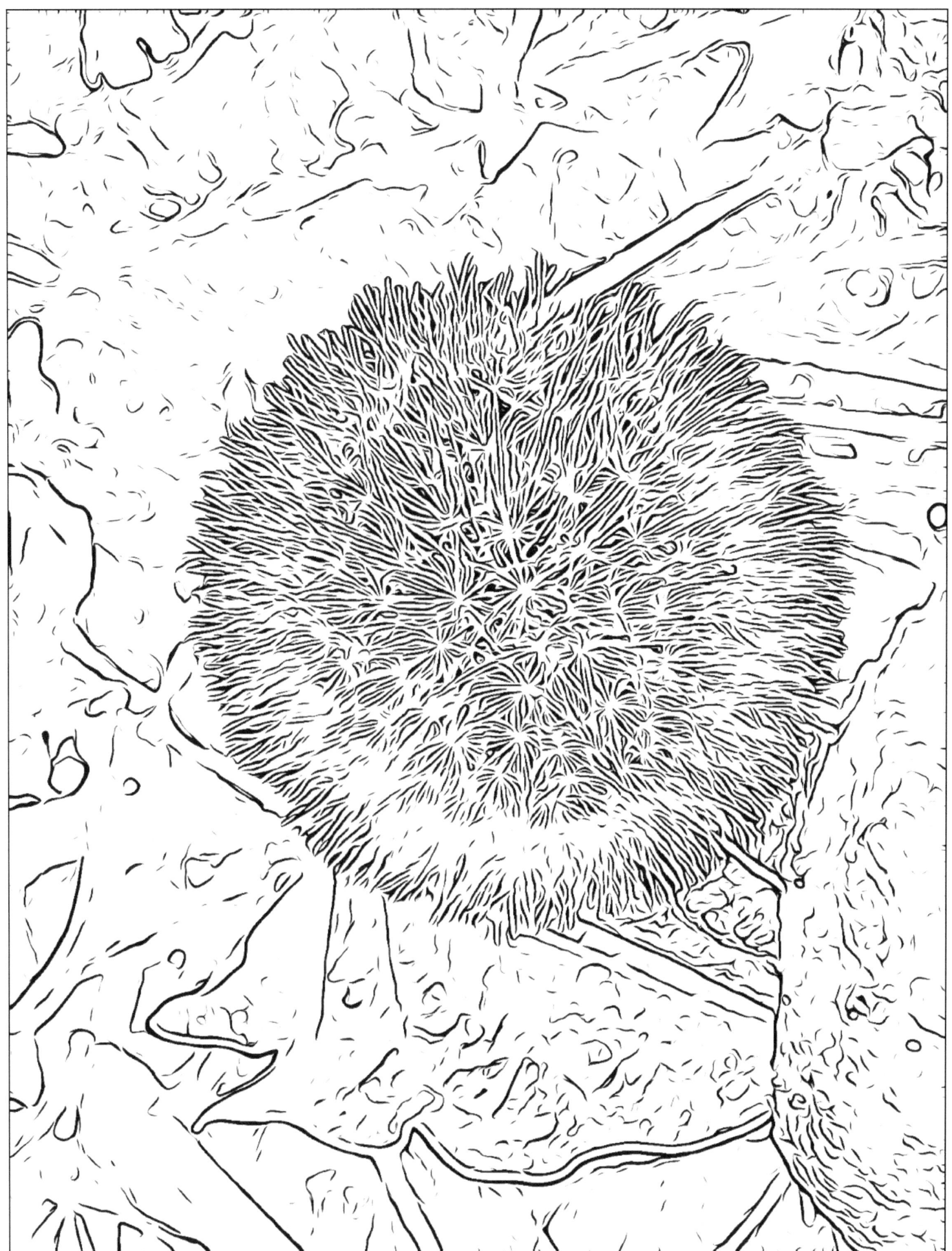

Color Test Area

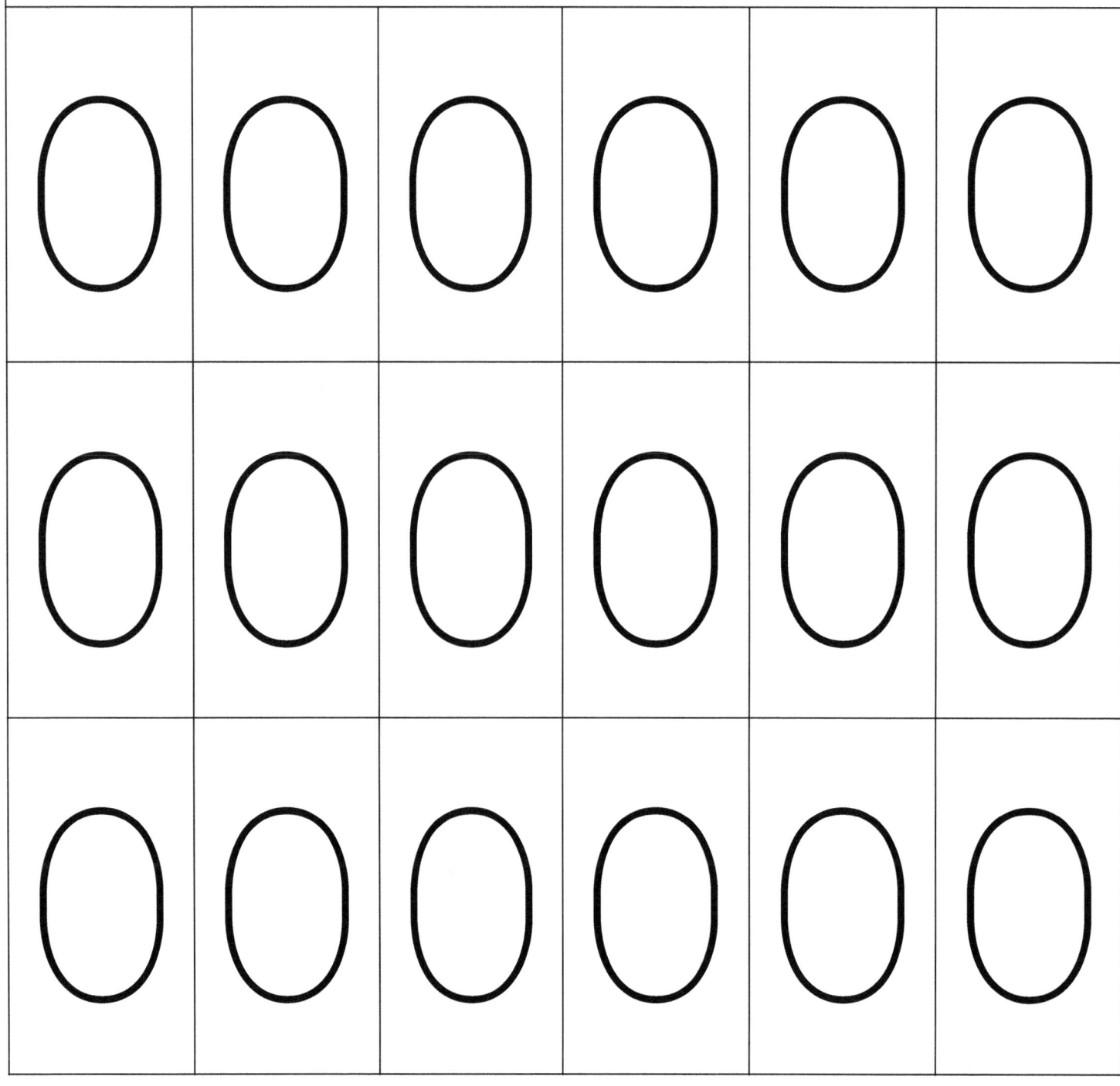

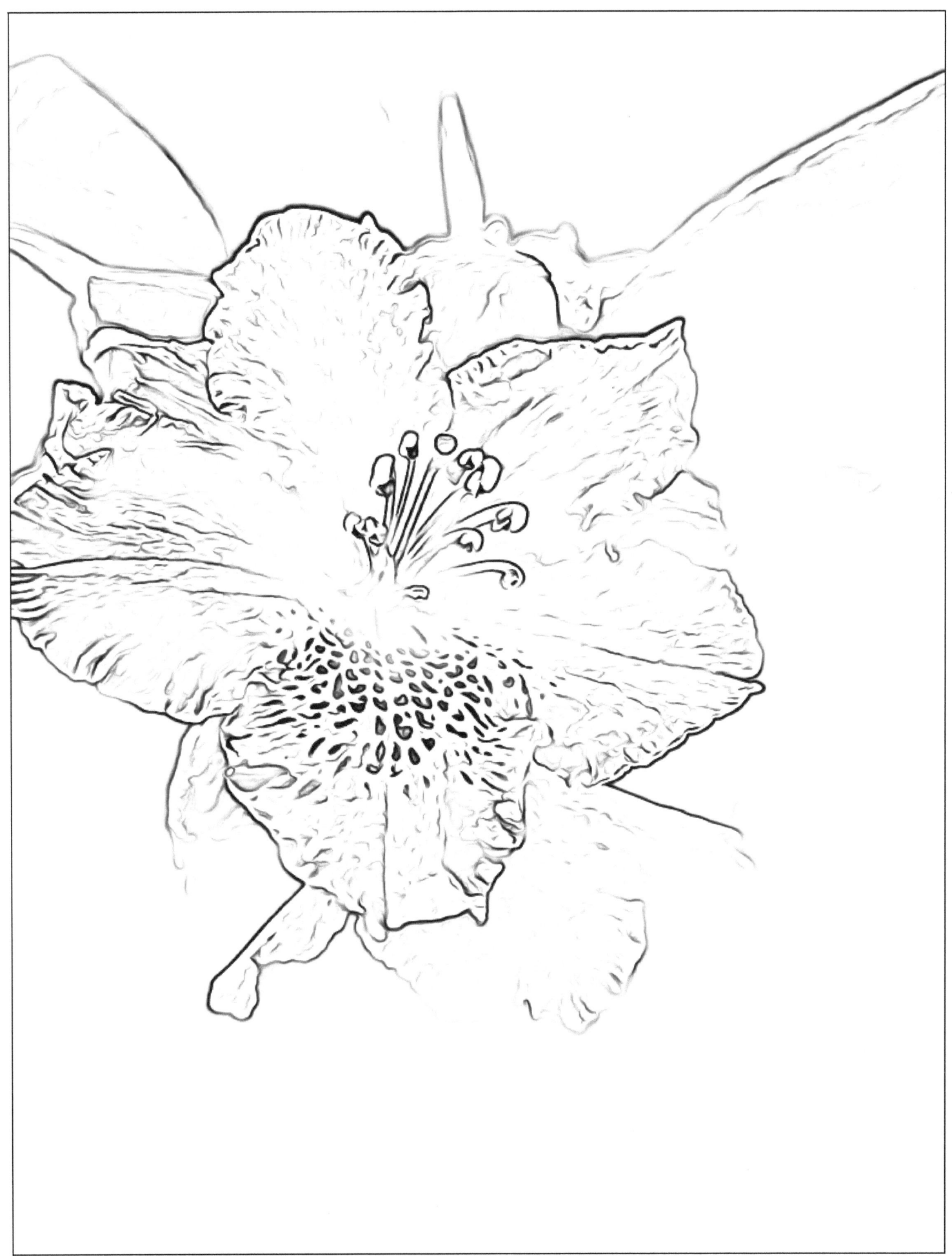

Color Test Area

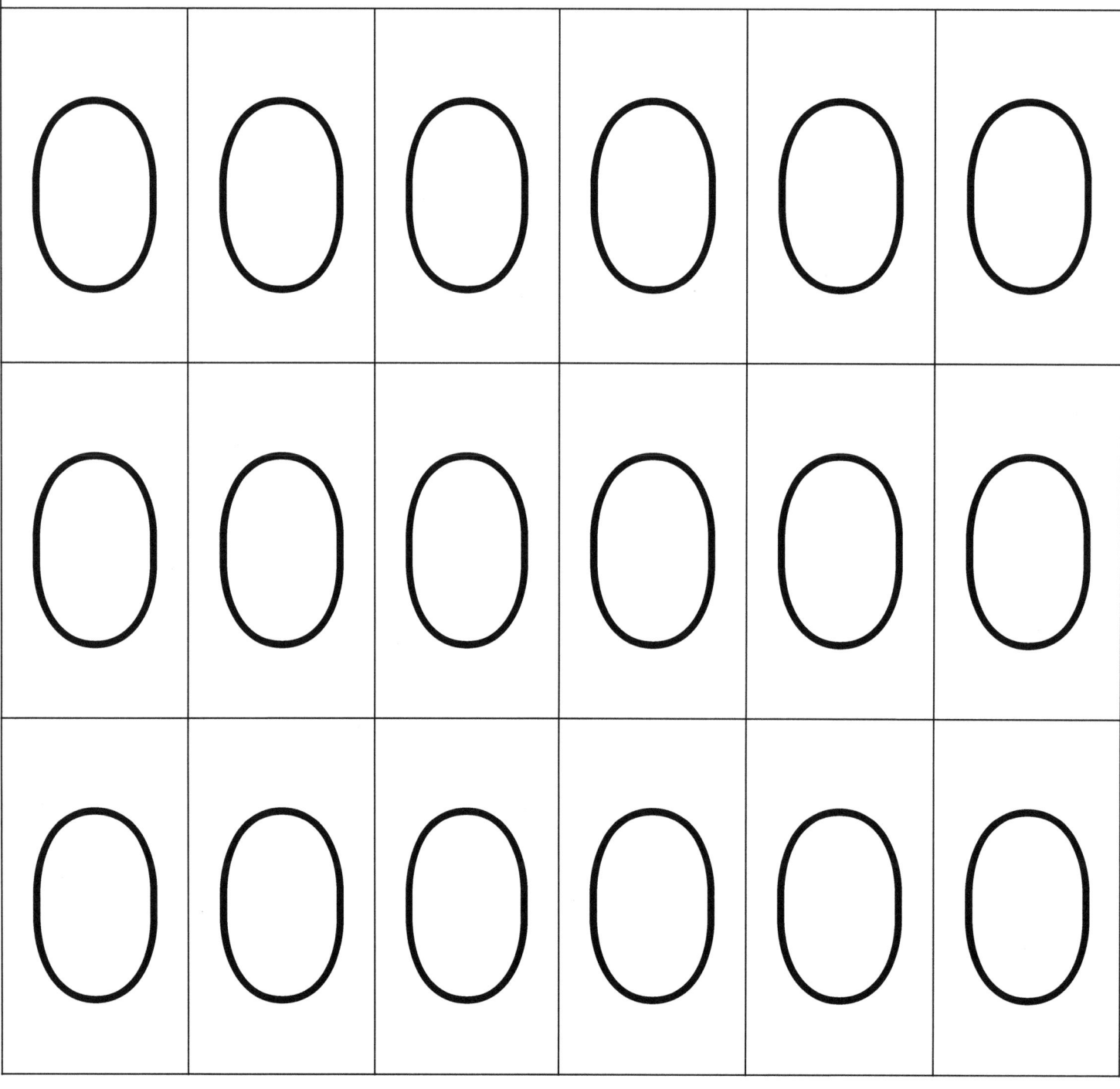

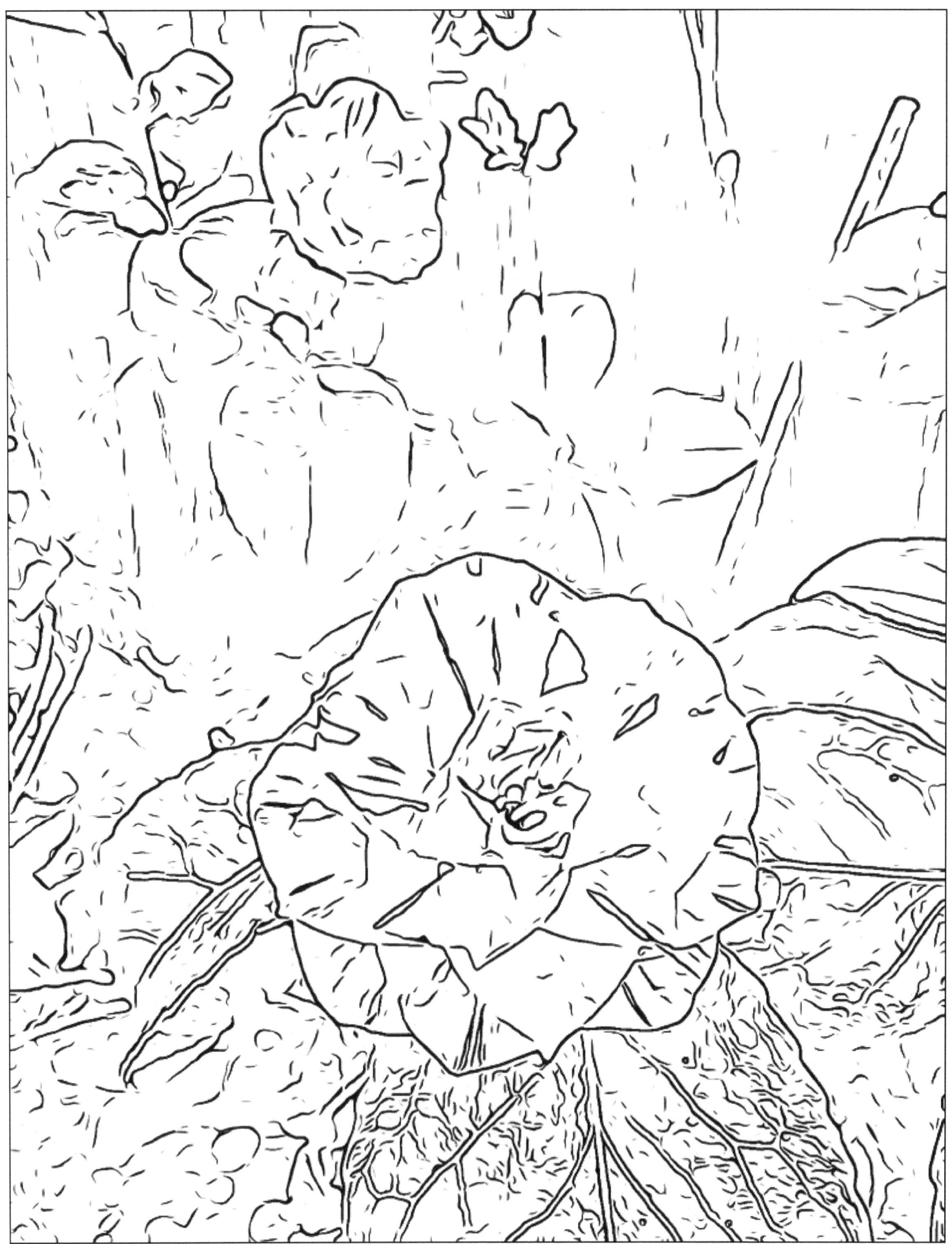

Color Test Area

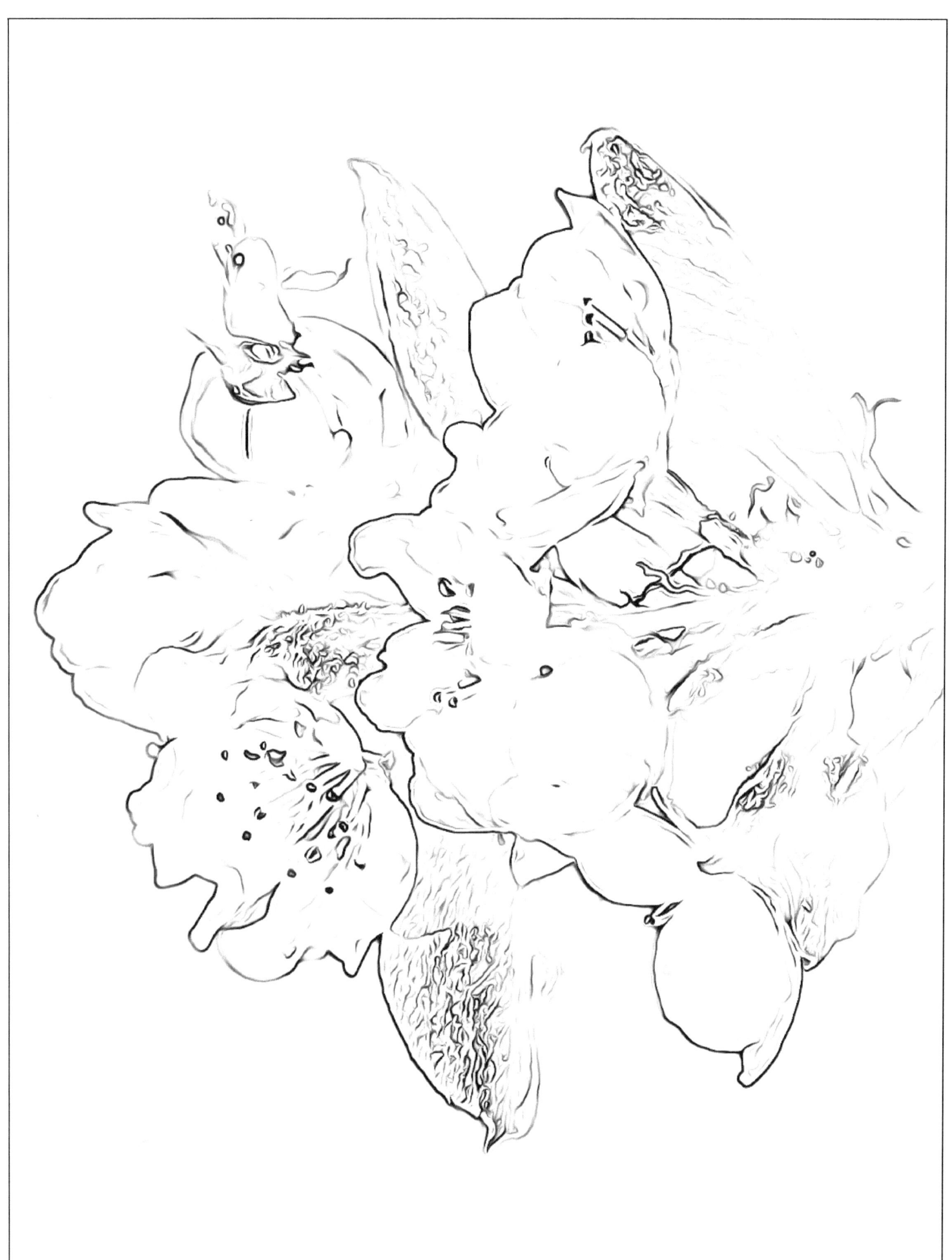

Color Test Area

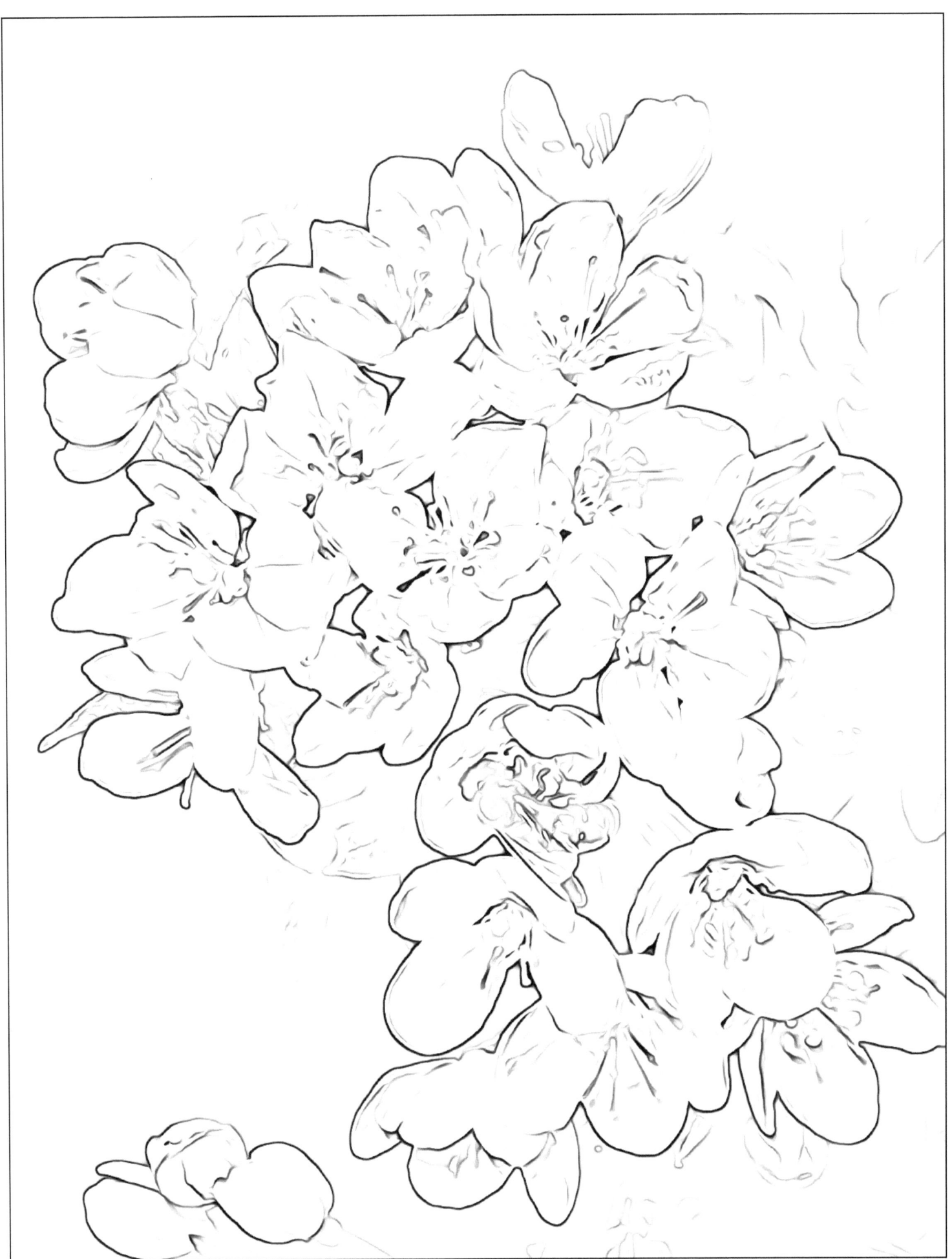

Color Test Area

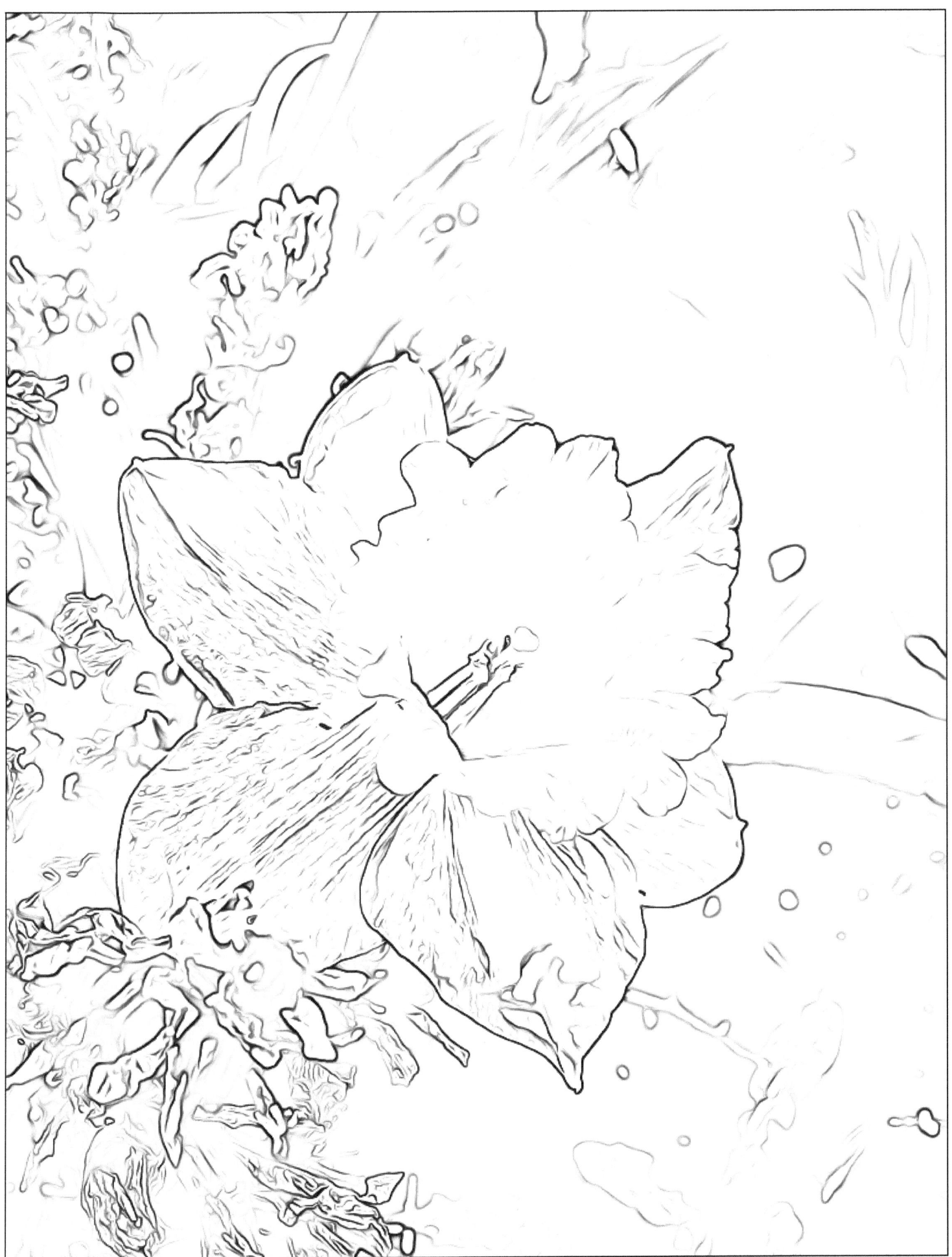

www.ingramcontent.com/pod-product-compliance
Lightning Source LLC
Chambersburg PA
CBHW040415220526
45473CB00004B/1250